50 PEOPLE WHO F***ED UP SOUTH AFRICA
THE LOST DECADE

Alexander Parker
& Tim Richman
with cartoons from the archive of
ZAPIRO

50 PEOPLE
WHO F***ED UP
SOUTH AFRICA
THE LOST DECADE

AlexanDer Parker
& Tim Richman
With cartoons from the archive of
ZAPIRO

Published by Mercury
an imprint of Burnet Media

Burnet Media is the publisher of Mercury and Two Dogs books
info@burnetmedia.co.za
www.burnetmedia.co.za
PO Box 53557, Kenilworth, 7745,
South Africa

First published 2020

This POD edition printed, bound and distributed
by Amazon
www.amazon.com

Also available as an ebook

To our families at the end of a helluva year.

ABOUT THE CONTRIBUTORS
Alexander Parker, **Tim Richman** and **Zapiro** are the team behind the previous three bestselling *50 People* titles: *50 People Who Stuffed Up South Africa* (2010), *50 Flippen Brilliant South Africans* (2012) and *50 People Who Stuffed Up The World* (2016).

Parker and Richman have authored a number of books between them. Zapiro is South Africa's premier cartoonist. His latest annual anthology is *Do The Macorona* (2020).

Contents

Introduction

Harold Wilson's observation that a week is a long time in politics is borne out time and again. Wilson, a British Prime Minister in the 1960s, would have been surveying the Westminster landscape. For our purposes, however, perhaps Lenin's take is a little closer to the bone: "There are decades where nothing happens, and there are weeks where decades happen."

In South Africa, you can have three finance ministers over a long weekend and corruption trials that last 20 years. It is fast and slow. It is impossible to keep up with and yet exasperatingly unchanged. It can be an exhausting place to live.

In many ways, therefore, a decade in the politics and cultural life of a nation is an arbitrary stretch of time. Why ten years and not 12, or eight? In the case of this unacademic work, we choose the "lost decade" because November 2020 happens to mark the tenth anniversary of the publication of *50 People Who Stuffed Up South Africa*, and because President Ramaphosa spoke overtly of "nine lost years" of state capture under Jacob Zuma, which we are happy to parlay into a neat decade here. Conveniently, our timeline is bookended by the hope and success of the 2010 Soccer World Cup and the devastation of the pandemic year, 2020.

Thus constrained, it's necessary to explain the purpose of this book. The 50 people who reside here are responsible for neither the condition of this country in 2010, nor the fundamental social and cultural currents that have made so much of what they've done possible. Indeed, that is an offensive notion. Those bad bastards are in the other book, which quite rightly begins with Jan van Riebeeck's arrival at the Cape of Good Hope and – rather elegantly, we think – waltzes through the eras of the VOC, of Dutch, trekker, British and Zulu expansionism, imperialism and colonialism, through to the founding of this nation as we know it now, the early Afrikaner nationalists and the apartheid regime that ruled, lest we forget, from 1948 until 1994. It also includes some of the early post-democratic stuffer-uppers.

South Africa has been forged for centuries in the relentless fire of governments that considered black people sub-human. Its inequalities, contradictions and structural imbalances have been baked-in under a hot sun for 350 years. Expecting wholesale structural change in a quarter of a century is not a little like wondering why the Tankwa Karoo isn't a verdant jungle after a good rainy season. It is important to remember this when those of us so frustrated by the unmet potential of what could be wish for everyone to "just move on".

This is not to deny that some truly terrible people exist within these pages, but it is to say that things might have been different for many of them had they not inherited a country that has been so roundly stuffed up. There are, we would estimate, not a few who might have gone on to greatness in other circumstances, though we would prefer they go on to jail right now.

In many ways, South Africa is undergoing a reckoning in which it seems reasonable to ask whether this was all such a good idea. This country was invented in 1910 by Jan Smuts and Louis Botha – two polymaths that fate would throw together, and who managed, through sheer force of personality, to persuade an unsure Britain and an unwilling post-South African War Afrikaner populace that this merger of erstwhile Boer republics and British colonies was a decent plan. Such was their hubris that nobody considered asking the black folk who would make up the majority in this new country.

The ANC was founded in 1912, but black resistance to white domination here is as old as the hills, and has been expressed variously from the banks of the Liesbeek to the great plain at Isandlwana, at Ncome/Blood River, and for decades on the eastern fringes of British encroachment in the lands of the Xhosa people.

And so, then, here we are, in this place at this time. Much of what ails South Africa marches in step with international trends. Inequality is increasingly heightened. The urban/rural divide is only going to widen. The bankers and the lawyers and the corporations are getting stupid-rich. Crony capitalism is alive and well, and its policemen are rotten. Extreme opinions compounded in online bubbles are the order of the day. Black people are generally still poor. White people are generally better off.

The discourse is legitimately angrier and more impatient, and for enlightenment on these topics we humbly direct you to read Francis Fukuyama's *Identity* and Oliver Bullough's *Moneyland*. We are in the midst of extraordinary global change, and explanations for this lie elsewhere.

But there is a distressingly tumultuous South African amplification of all this fraught political upheaval. The 50 people in this book may not have been responsible for the state of the country in 2010, let alone in 1994, but they're still here for good reason. As in the original book, many of them are representatives of the particular crime they have committed, often one of very many in a contested space, and there are countless more who might have appeared here. Narrowing down the list was impossibly tricky, and you may well be disappointed by the absence of one of your pet peeves.

Either way, President Ramaphosa pretty much nailed it when he described the waste of the Zuma Years, his presence at the man's right hand through so much of it notwithstanding. In the dystopian, compassion-free wasteland that is social media, two things can never be true at once; in reality, as we try to make clear, that is so often the key to understanding. South Africa was saved by the ANC and South Africa is being destroyed by the ANC. Our economic salvation lies in the free enterprise of South Africans and yet too many businesses continue to behave appallingly. Taxpayers are justifiably livid at seeing their hard-earned contributions stolen, yet they are often loath to acknowledge their extraordinary good luck – what some might call their privilege – to be in a position to pay meaningful amounts of tax. Intergenerational wealth is just fine, but intergenerational poverty is not.

What's certain is that the people in this book have done great damage to a country that was already struggling. Their greatest collective crime is the squandering of hope and potential. This is an indignant book, as befits the times, because moving towards a better future is the foundation of civilisation and functional society. The lost decade was a decade of disappointment and disillusionment, to be sure, but we do discern light on the horizon.

It is too glib to simply claim the ongoing resilience of the average South African as a sturdiness unique to our people. It is infuriating, patronising and lazy – a classic trope of South African exceptionalism. People survive as best they can often in terrible circumstances, and they die too young.

It is the duty of the rest of us to make things better.

We are – just about – still a going concern. We are still a great-country-in-waiting. We are a ragtag assortment of disparate peoples from wildly diverse and varying backgrounds. It is our greatest strength and our greatest challenge. Most of us are good and decent. But, politics being what it is, the real bad buggers have found their way into power. South Africa can survive but things need to change – and while we can all agree that these 50 bastards are the first who need to go, that will be only the start. Let us understand what they've done. Let us call them out and call them names, where we must, because catharsis is necessary after times of darkness and abuse.

Afterwards, the rest is up to us.

Shaun Abrahams

b. March 1977

*National Director of Public Prosecutions (2015-2018); one
in a long line of politically compromised public prosecutors;
sheep in a wolf's job; wide-eyed, bushy-browed hand
of the state capturers*

*Dishonourable mentions: the Guptas, Nomgcobo Jiba,
Lawrence Mrwebi, Berning Ntlemeza, Jacob Zuma*

THE OLD-FASHIONED WAY OF STAGING a coup goes like this.

Arrest whichever president-for-life scumbag is currently residing
in the big house.
Seize control of the broadcasters.
Seize control of the airport and the borders.

Simple, really, in a time before social media. Then all you had to do was appear on Radio Failed State to assure the masses that this was a democratic revolution and elections could be expected sometime before the next ice age.

State capture is different in that there are fewer guns involved. It's a bloodless route to the same place, and it can be done, as South Africans have come to realise over the course of the last decade, even in a democracy with a complex economy such as ours. This way, instead of over-running the broadcaster with AK-wielding soldiers, it's more effective to just buy the guy who's running it. *(See Hlaudi Motsoeneng.)* There are, however, rather a few more institutions that need to be acquired for maximum effect. In a functioning democracy designed as carefully as South Africa's, the prospective capturers must ensure they have positioned all the right people in all the right places to be able to optimise their looting. It is a painstaking and costly process. Make one mistaken appointment in the constellation of corruption – Advocate Thuli Madonsela as Public Protector, for example – and it can set back the programme dramatically.

The junta of Jacob Zuma and his managers, the Guptas, didn't just take over the state broadcaster; they created their own broadcaster, along with a newspaper, and made friends with an entire media house. *(See The Guptas and Iqbal Survé.)* To pay the bills, it was important to get going on the looting early, and they made easy inroads into state-operated entities such as Eskom and SAA. *(See Brian Molefe and Dudu Myeni.)* Then, having stolen the money, it was obviously critical to avoid tax liabilities on the loot – so the revenue service was another expensive and necessary acquisition. *(See Tom Moyane.)* The demoralised and overwhelmed police force was relatively easy to handle, but a real challenge came with the prosecutors.

Prosecutors who did their job would have scuppered the state capture project, which could only go ahead if the law wasn't applied to the thieves. Thus, owning the National Prosecuting Authority (NPA) was a strategic priority. Those who did could look down their noses and imperiously say that they understood the division of powers in a democratic country, and that any complaints of corruption should be left to "the relevant authorities" – all along knowing that the relevant authorities were wholly owned entities of State Capture Pty Ltd.

The judiciary was far more difficult to own or influence *(see John Hlophe)*, but was perhaps not necessary. As much as Zuma may have understood that his actions with the NPA would eventually go through the commission-of-inquiry legal-challenge endless-appeals merry-go-round, there was an instinctive realisation that using state companies and departments to shovel enormous truckloads of swag into the Guptas' Dubai bank accounts is way faster than a legal process in South Africa.

And so we start proceedings here, in our potted review of the disastrous 2010s, with the battle for ownership of the NPA.

Readers may not remember much about Judge Christopher Nicholson, a once highly regarded jurist who had worked in small ways to undo some of apartheid's more abhorrent laws, and in smaller ways to undo its manifestations – he founded Natal's first non-racial cricket club, for example. But in the post-democratic era he dealt the country a blow that has wrought unfathomable damage. It was South Africa's misfortune that he was the man in the robes who dismissed Jacob Zuma's corruption charges in 2008 on procedural grounds. In his absolutely incendiary judgment, the consequences of which we are still reeling from today, he held that the prosecutors had experienced "baleful political influence".

Nicholson's judgment was eventually thrown out – ripped apart, in fact, by the Supreme Court of Appeal – but the damage had been done. Mbeki was out. Zuma was in. As columnist William Saunderson-Meyer observed, "Zuma and his populist cabal had parlayed the Nicholson ruling into a toxic presidency that would run for nine miserable years before ending in national ignominy and ruin." Quite so.

In the possibly uneducated view of these authors, it seems that both Nicholson and the Supreme Court were looking at the same quandary from different sides. They were both right in a way, but they were both also disastrously wrong. As Saunderson-Meyer wrote, "Does anyone seriously doubt that Mbeki – be it overtly or with a nudge and a wink

– influenced successive NPA heads to either prosecute or withhold prosecution, according to what best benefited him and the ANC?"

Either way, with Mbeki unceremoniously booted out, Zuma moonwalked with characteristic style from the High Court to Tuynhuis, and he was sworn in as President of South Africa in May 2009. Let us be perfectly clear: more evil thugs have inhabited those storied walls; nevertheless, this was the last damn thing South Africa needed, and after half a year's settling in the stage was set for the decade to come.

To be sure, then, Zuma's presidency started in an environment in which politics had for years very clearly shaped events at the NPA. Funny, for example, that when head prosecutor Vusi Pikoli wanted to execute a warrant of arrest against President Mbeki's catastrophically hopeless National Police Commissioner Jackie Selebi, it should suddenly be deemed that he had suffered an irretrievable breakdown of his relationship with the Minister of Justice, Brigitte Mabandla, and find himself out on his ear. So we shouldn't make the mistake of thinking that Zuma invented the idea of meddling with the NPA. The thing with Zuma was the shamelessness.

In the decade that concerns this book, the NPA has had four full-time national directors and three acting national directors to connect them. After a wrangle to get rid of Pikoli, there followed Zuma's appointment in 2009 of Menzi Simelane, who somehow staggered through three years before a court found his appointment to be invalid. It was clear to anyone who'd ever read a book that Simelane was a poor choice, but what followed really blew the mind. Next, Mxolisi Nxasana filled the role. This turned out to be a regrettable choice for Zuma, because in 2014 Nxasana dared to do his job and reinstate criminal charges against former crime intelligence boss Richard Mdluli. The Mdluli saga was one of those long-running ANC factional-fighting sub-plots that would eventually see the guy being sentenced to jail in 2020, all of 22 years after the fact. Back in 2014, though, he was Zuma's man, and reinstating criminal charges against him just wasn't on, so, in the way of any good spymaster, Zuma used the dirt he had on Nxasana to move him along. In this instance, he had undisclosed convictions for assault and was once acquitted, on the basis of self-defence, of murder. Not exactly NPA-leading material. Nxasana was paid R17 million to bugger off without too much hassle, and in June 2015, Zuma, to the surprise of even those most cynical about the perpetually politicised nature of the NPA, appointed one Shaun Abrahams to head the NPA.

Well, no mistakes this time.

Abrahams was a mid-level prosecutor with 17 years' experience. He was 39, he had the authority of a wet rag, and he was set to be the head clown of Zuma's tragic little circus.

Shaun the Sheep, as he came to be known, was complicit not only in the worst of state capture, but also in the gutting of the NPA, which shed committed and talented lawyers as they watched the institution collapse around them. The fact that there is only now, as we type these words in late 2020, any sign of a recovery at the NPA illustrates the severity of the harm that was done.

As head of the country's ultimate prosecuting authority, Abrahams was mandated to work closely with Berning Ntlemeza, head of the country's ultimate criminal investigation authority, the Hawks. Whereas Abrahams had flown under the radar, Ntlemeza was a walking controversy, closely connected to Mdluli, among others, and described by the Pretoria High Court as "biased and dishonest" and lacking "integrity and honour".

Together, they stood by and watched as the Guptas and the Zumas built a pathway paved with stolen South African gold, all the way to Dubai. This much was laid out in clearly actionable black-and-white glory as detailed analyses of the Gupta Leaks emails, from May 2017 onwards,

> "Prosecutors who stood for justice and who prosecuted without 'fear or favour' were systematically worked out and replaced by pliable prosecutors who acted towards political objectives and not in the interests of justice."
>
> *Former KZN Hawks head Johan Booysen, Zondo commission affidavit*

the work of a team of investigative journalists literally connecting the dots for any willing prosecutors.

Yet Abrahams and co did nothing as the state capturers destroyed SAA, ruined Transnet and utterly, completely trashed Eskom. And, as they say in the Verimark ads, that's not all! The standing aside was one thing, but charging a sitting finance minister with fraud was a new level even for the NPA…

In 2015, after the Nenegate debacle, South Africa found itself in the wholly embarrassing situation of having had three ministers of finance in five days. *(See Des van Rooyen.)* For Zuma, the ANC state capture crew and its running dogs, the EFF, the real nub of the problem was that the third one was Pravin Gordhan. This was not part of the plan. In his previous stint as finance minister, Gordhan had shown a disappointing reluctance to hand the keys to the treasury to the Gupta/Gucci mafia, and it wouldn't do to have him back there for long. Zuma must have been running short of ideas – until he realised he had a pet sheep at the NPA.

And that's how Shaun Abrahams ended up presiding over a prosecuting authority that charged a sitting finance minister with fraud in October 2016, just days before he was due to give his mid-term budget statement. And it was Abrahams who strode on as half a trillion rand of value was wiped off South African companies and the rand fell to historic lows against other currencies. It was Abrahams who bleated so terribly unconvincingly that he was operating absolutely independently and without any political interference whatsoever, as South Africa pitched inevitably toward the realm of junk status. It was Abrahams who put his signature on a charge sheet of politically motivated fantasy that told the outside world that this is not a serious country any more, so get your money out while you can.

And they did.

Elsewhere, Abrahams conspired with advocate Nomgcobo Jiba and others to implicate head of the Hawks in KwaZulu-Natal, Johan Booysen, along with his men, in tales of murder and police brutality in and around Durban. Their involvement was one element of the notorious

Cato Manor disinformation campaign, another exhausting saga that dragged out over much of the decade, initially in the *Sunday Times* and ultimately in the courts. Booysen had made the mistake of trying to do his job in Zuma family territory, but he was eventually vindicated in 2019 by the withdrawal of charges against him by Abrahams's successor Shamila Batohi.

By this stage, Abrahams had followed the lead of so many NPA heads before him: booted out of the job by a court. His appointment was found to be invalid due to the unconstitutional manner in which his predecessor had been winkled from the job, and in August 2018 he was despatched to pastures new. Jiba and fellow NPA prosecutor Lawrence Mrwebi, both steeped in disgrace and found to be unfit for the positions, followed suit.

For a sense of what might have motivated these highly qualified, lowly moralised individuals, consider that Jiba, who had been acting NDPP in 2012, was the wife of a man who had had his criminal record expunged, in 2010, by none other than Jacob Zuma. Quite what Zuma had on Shaun Abrahams, we don't know – but it must have been a whopper.

Batohi is on record as describing the rot that Abrahams had left as "much worse than I expected". We doubt she was expecting a picnic.

It's safe to say that Batohi is no Shaun the Sheep. But will she ever clean up the mess he left behind?

Adam Catzavelos

b. 28 December 1978

*Viral racist; not representative of the average
South African; just what we don't need*

WELL, THERE IT IS. Some Joburg non-entity with his Bedfordview accent telling us how much he loves the beach he's on because there's "not a k****r in sight", and then recording it at the ideal length for social media distribution. Like South Africa needs these grotesque distractions.

In August 2018, Adam Catzavelos filmed himself saying these words while on holiday in Greece:

"Let me give you a weather forecast here. Blue skies, beautiful day, amazing sea, and not one k***** in sight, fucken heaven on earth. You cannot beat this. You cannot beat this."

Then he pressed send.

The suppurating racism aside, what a very weird way to live. Something must be broken inside a person if he flies halfway around the world, walks onto a pristine beach and chooses to focus not on it being very lovely, not on it being very beautiful, but hey, look, there are no black people here!

Living with this level of racism must be so onerous. The cognitive cartwheels required to pile just about every damn thing, including a Greek beach, onto this particular hobby horse must be like some kind of debilitating mental illness.

But Adam Catzavelos isn't ill. He's just an intergalactic loser, the kind of moron who creates a click-fest spectacle on *TimesLive* and hands political race-baiters like Mbuyiseni Ndlozi and his friends at the EFF some more 95-unleaded for the flames.

Catzavelos would appear to have grown up in the security of a family business. He would appear to have never really struggled. And then he does this god-awful thing to his black compatriots, the overwhelming majority of whom struggle every day.

The Institute of Race Relations runs regular surveys that consistently show most South Africans to be reasonable and decent people. Most of us believe race relations have improved since 1994. Most of us want to live and let live. People like Adam Catzavelos, Vicki Momberg and Penny Sparrow, and their whites-hating equivalents, really do represent a sliver of society today. This lot, however, feel compelled to express to the world their prejudices, where they are amplified online and in the media by those who thrive on race-based controversy. In doing what they do, they directly affect our political discourse.

These days, the law rightly catches up with people like Catzavelos. In February 2020 he pleaded guilty to crimen injuria, and received a suspended sentence and R50,000 fine, on top of an earlier settlement agreement that saw him fined R150,000 and doing community service in Orlando, Soweto. Momberg, the notorious racist estate agent, got two years in the banger.

Perhaps, then, we should leave the final word to Nic Catzavelos, Adam's brother. In announcing that Adam's shares in the family business had been transferred to its staff, he said, "He made a video that is obscenely racist, which speaks for itself. There is no way the video could be taken out of context. You cannot wrap this up in cotton wool." And of the fury directed at the Catzavelos family and their business, he said, "Who wouldn't be angry? It's despicable, and given our country's history, it's completely understandable."

South Africa needs more Nic Catzaveloses and fewer Adam Catzaveloses. Still, all these years later, they are a poison in our society.

Adri Senekal de Wet

*Executive editor of Business Report; the polar opposite
of journalistic integrity; face of the critical media battle
between good and evil*

THESE DAYS IT DOESN'T TAKE TOO MANY CONVERSATIONS in the
Johannesburg northern suburbs or Cape Town southern suburbs to
work out that many South Africans who have the means are "looking for
opportunities overseas". Over the past few years the topic of emigration
has drifted from taboo to *de rigueur*, taking the dinner-party top spot
held by "why I bant/don't bant" earlier in the decade. In the first quarter
of 2019, the FNB Estate Agents Survey reported that 14.2% of all its
property sales were the result of families – and taxpayers – leaving the
country. In 2020, emigration specialists Henley & Partners reported a
near 50% increase in South Africans looking to move abroad in the first
half of the year. Numbers to give the bean counters at SARS more than
a few palpitations.

Many of those who have not yet emigrated but will do so in the coming years have "emotionally emigrated". They've stopped reading the news that doesn't immediately affect them; stopped worrying about the plight of the poor and the state of the country's finances. When something is broken beyond repair, you avert your gaze and look elsewhere.

But there are those among us made of sterner stuff. Those who continue to have hope. Those who continue to read the news…

Journalists are a strange breed. It's a calling, no doubt. The money is terrible; the Gucci-clad, AMG-driving ordure running the country will despise you; and the trolls, bots, racists, liars and conspiracy theorists will come for you in their digital droves. If you're a woman, you can expect some added misogyny from the EFF.

The fact that we can write a book such as this one is down to the best of this breed.

In the grander scheme, this book is hardly important, but the state of our democracy is, and the facts in this book are now free for dissemination for two reasons. First, because of the bravery of the old, long-dead liberation ANC that chucked media censorship in the bin three decades ago (worth remembering). And, second, because of the work of some relentlessly brave and unflaggingly dogged journalists. They are too many to mention, but where would we be without these modern heroes?

Adriaan Basson
Terry Bell
Jessica Bezuidenhout
Branko Brkic
Stefaans Brümmer
Susan Comrie
Vincent Cruywagen
Pieter Du Toit
Lionel Faull
Stephen Grootes
Ferial Haffajee
Ed Herbst

Andisiwe Makinana
Mondli Makhanya
Justice Malala
Sikonathi Mantshantsha
Karyn Maughan
Craig McKune
Pieter-Louis Myburgh
Bronwyn Nortje
Khadija Patel
Carol Paton
Richard Poplak
Micah Reddy
Sam Sole
Tabelo Timse
Marianne Thamm
Mandy Wiener
Dewald van Rensburg
Pauli Van Wyk
Songezo Zibi

Then, especially in the context of "the lost decade" of the Zuma Years, there is the granddaddy of reportage: Jacques Pauw, investigative journalist and author of *The President's Keepers*, a book that sold more than 200,000 copies and single-handedly shifted our political dial.

Most of those listed above worked on the game-changing Gupta Leaks. Some are brave analysts who say the things in public forums that need to be said. Together, they represent a broad ideological spectrum without extremities, which is as it should be. But they are hardly flawless. Between them, they have courted controversy, been accused of naivety *and* cynicism, faced justified criticism, held opinions that didn't stand the test of time, misjudged their marks and had to issue corrections, all while making questionable fashion decisions. Such is the path to tread of the committed journalist, but ultimately they are the truth tellers whose work has directly and positively influenced the unfolding of our recent history.

At the other end of the scale, however, the media has played its part in our parlous state as well.

In his recent book *So, For The Record*, media veteran Anton Harber describes the Guptas' New Age Media, Iqbal Survé's Sekunjalo Independent Media and the SABC as "direct examples of the growing phenomenon of media capture, where the media lost their autonomy and their ability to act with a will of their own, and their primary function of informing the public became secondary to servicing vested interests". This is a polite way of saying that these three institutions – one dead, one dying, one now possibly resurrected – have been stuffed to hell and back by the megalomaniacs who run them. We'll get to the key actors in all three in the pages to come.

Elsewhere, the major media houses have battled to adapt in a decade in which every hand clutching a smartphone has become its own publisher, often on multiple platforms. Mass-readership news websites here have fallen, as they have around the world, for the Google Ads-driven spiral of doom, chasing clicks for cash. Hence underpaid junior editors read something on their Twitter, believe it to be "news", rehash it as "Mzansi reacts to [insert Twitter outrage *du jour*]", tweet it out and watch the merry-go-round. If that fails, give Julius Malema some more publicity.

Kudos, then, to the likes of *Daily Maverick* for pioneering a subscription model that's generating reader trust, global acclaim and actual revenue, and even to *News24* for daring to partially go behind a paywall in 2020.

Our media houses have faced a real battle during the state capture years – from the online tech onslaught, from the state capturers and, in some ways most disappointingly, from journalists who have fallen prey to the disinformation game and becomes its disseminators.

Some of the most prominent cock-ups have occurred at the *Sunday Times* which, because of its power and reach, found itself particularly vulnerable to the efforts of ANC factions to discredit each other. Top reporters should be savvy enough to avoid the traps, however, and the *Sunday Times* has published some really damaging drivel, notably about the SARS "rogue unit" (air cover designed to protect the looters at SARS), the "Cato Manor death squad" (nonsense designed to protect Zuma and friends from difficult SAPS investigations) and, weirdly, a front-page splash about the sea around Cape Town being sold to China (just nonsense). All hugely damaging, and there are journalists whose good names will never recover from this.

But by far the worst thing to come out of media in the past decade is the phenomenon known as Adri Senekal de Wet. Journalists are, as we've seen, as flawed as everyone else. They can be corrupt and they can be naive. Altogether too many are activists masquerading as analysts. They quite naturally bring their own anger and guilt and bias and prejudice to their work. They're human. Adri Senekal de Wet, however, is like nothing our world of journalism has seen before.

De Wet was once Sekunjalo Investment Holdings' "stakeholder relations executive". That is, she was Iqbal Survé's spin doctor, which made her an obvious choice to take over as "executive editor" of *Business Report*, the business and finance daily distributed with Independent titles, including *The Star, Cape Times, The Mercury* and *Pretoria News*.

Business Report used to matter. It may have played second fiddle to *Business Day*, but its reach and sheer circulation made it an important publication for those watching the traditional economy and the political economy. While continuing to retain good reporters who were, privately, aghast and horrified at what was going on around them, De Wet set about to be chief arse-kisser of her boss, his companies and their various creative adventures in corporate finance.

Anybody who's spent any time in a real newsroom will tell you that at the absolute best there is little respect for the paper's owners. It's why good newspapers work, and the business owners and managers generally steer clear of the newsroom as you would a nest of cobras. Independent Media no longer produces good newspapers. Under Survé, it has come to resemble a cult. Those who could see it for what it is were fired or ran for the hills. Those who fell for it, fell hard – like De Wet and fellow Independent editors Gasant Abarder and Aneez Salie.

De Wet refers in bizarre glowing terms to her leader as "Doc", and appears to have pitched for her *Business Report* position with a 3,500-

word "open letter" she wrote to him, supposedly out of the blue, in 2016.

"My only link with you today is that I am one of your 5,000 FB friends," she wrote, in case anyone might dare to think this was a paid-for PR spiel. "I think if FB did not have a 5,000 limit you would have a million friends by now?"

Then: "Dr Survé, when I read the latest articles about you, I have to ask myself, why aren't you reacting? This is ridiculous! How can ANYBODY question YOU?"

The letter goes on and on – you can almost smell the brown-nosing through the screen; she barely comes up for air – but that, in a nutshell, appears to be the editorial approach she has subsequently adopted for *Business Report*. (If it was a job application, she nailed it!)

De Wet sealed her fate as the anti-journalist with an incoherent attack on veteran investigative reporter Sam Sole after he exposed Survé's laughable attempt to extract billions out of investors with the public offering of his hollow entity Sagarmatha Technologies. Despite De Wet's hare-brained attempts to spin the offering as an "African unicorn" and

Dear Adri Senekal de Wet,
I do realise that, as editor of *Business Report*, one of Independent's stable of publications, you have to sing for your supper and that is why you so often leap with alacrity to the defence of your boss, Dr Iqbal Survé.

I also realise that – given the one-sided way you and your publications have covered (and continue to cover) the issue of government pensioners' money being channelled to Survé and his companies in circumstances best described as questionable – you would not recognise real journalism if it bit you in the bum...

You, Adri, will end up on the wrong side of history. You may not realise this, but karma is not a brand of margarine.

Brendan Seery, 2019

> "South Africa, we have a problem. There is a move afoot in the country that is potentially far more dangerous than the Guptas' attempted takeover of the country, and that is media manipulation and unethical reporting designed to prevent broader economic participation."
>
> *Independent Media editorial, apparently written by Adri Senekal de Wet as she battled the irony gods, April 2018*

her boss as the next Jeff Bezos, Sagarmatha collapsed under the weight of its own internal vacuum.

Unique as she may be, Adri Senekal de Wet represents the dark temptations our journalists face and often can't resist. No doubt she will continue to heap praise onto her boss on the single-ply known as *Business Report*. Follow the incentive, and say a prayer for the real journalists still out there.

Wouldn't it be lovely if the likes of Adri emigrated?

See Jack Dorsey, The Guptas, Hlaudi Motsoeneng, Iqbal Survé.

Bathabile Dlamini

b. 10 September 1962

*Minister of Social Development (2010-2018); Minister
of Women in the Presidency (2018-2019); Leader of the
ANC Women's League (still!); gormless face of government
indifference; giver-away of the government game*

"All of us have our smallanyana skeletons"
—BATHABILE DLAMINI, 2016

RESIGNATION

PROSECUTION for criminal misconduct

LUMKA OLIPHANT, SPOKESPERSON FOR BATHABILE DLAMINI, went beyond the usual polite rejoinders to criticism of her principal when she suggested in January 2017 that upbraiding Dlamini for her politics was fine, but that otherwise people shouldn't "talk shit about her".

This was in response to claims that Dlamini, erstwhile social development minister, was drunk on the job once again. She has since claimed to suffer from epilepsy, and that her medication had recently been changed.

Drunk or not, there's enough video evidence of the minister appearing to be "unsteady on her feet", as they say. Either way, Bathabile Dlamini's real crimes are not her alleged drunkenness or even the scale of her corruption. To use her own phrase, given the magnitude of the looting going on around her, her contribution was "smallanyana" stuff. A couple of hundred grand pilfered so she could holiday on the public purse. A million bucks or thereabouts of South African Social Security Agency (Sassa) money blown on her children's security detail. A billion or so of irregular expenditure by the agency itself.

One of the remarkable things about Bathabile Dlamini is that she is a senior member of the ANC who has actually been prosecuted for graft. We can only assume somebody buggered up there – they didn't even lose the docket! – because she was forced to plead guilty to fraud involving R254,000 in 2006. She was sentenced to a R120,000 fine or five years' imprisonment with an additional five-year suspended sentence – this was as part of the Travelgate scandal for the now quaint-sounding crime of using parliamentary vouchers intended for air travel to pay for extras like hotel accommodation and whatnot. Just a cheeky little holiday on us, you see.

Still, small beer. Entry-level stuff for the Zuma era. Nothing to frighten the horses at treasury. She's on our list for something else, then.

As social development minister, Dlamini was supposed to oversee one of the most critical of day-to-day functions of the government. It's not a function that gets too much mileage at middle-class dinner parties and it doesn't keep the economists up all night. But concerned South Africans were extremely worried that when tasked with transferring the job of paying out social grants from Cash Paymaster Services to the state, she appeared to be too busy being unsteady on her feet at the One & Only hotel in Cape Town to bother to get it done.

Some facts are required here. First, we're not going to whinge about taxpayers' money as if taxpayers are the primary victims of the theft of state funds. It is money supplied by taxpayers, but the victims are the poorest of the poor. Dlamini's stays at hotels between June 2009 and August 2011 cost the most vulnerable people in our country three quarters of a million rand.

Oliphant would haughtily claim that this was necessary as "the very nature of the minister's work is working with the poor, who are in very rural areas of the country and which require her to be constantly out of the office together with her staff".

Okay, fair's fair. As much as you might hold Dlamini in disdain for her unsteadiness of foot, she surely deserves reasonable accommodation as she ranges across the land executing her solemn duty. As when she visited the impoverished communities in the remote rural hinterland that is Green Point, Cape Town without suitable accommodation. Teeming as it is with herds of untamed German tourists and hardened gangs of Bantry Bay teenagers armed with fully-automatic gelatos, it explains, we feel, 53 nights (as in fifty-three nights, nearly eight straight weeks) in the Radisson Blu Hotel, 26 nights in the Westin Grand Arabella Quays, and the five nights where she was really forced to slum it with the rurals at the One & Only.

As the minister contemplated her pillow menu, too exhausted to traipse the distance to her ministerial Cape Town accommodation literally several kilometres away, one wonders if her assertion in 2016 that R753 a month was enough for a person to live off created a little dissonance. Or did the unsteady feet ensure such difficult thoughts didn't keep the minister up at night? We will probably never know.

In any case, the quantum of the cash isn't why Dlamini is here. If this book was graded on the simple basis of how much money people stole – or, if you prefer, spent irregularly – Dlamini probably wouldn't have made the top 500. She is here for being a particularly good example of the odd mixture of incompetence, greed and that most egregious of political crimes, indifference.

It's the not-giving-a-damn that sticks in the craw. Imagine being put in a position to do something that will fundamentally improve the lives of 45% of South African households. A position in which the decisions you make can really help 17 million people. Those of us who do ordinary jobs take some solace in the idea that we contribute to society with charitable work and donations, and through our limited economic activity and the taxes we pay. But to literally be the minister of Social Development, the individual whose work it is to pay our poor compatriots the money they need to feed themselves? It's hard, in all honesty, to imagine a greater privilege and a weightier task.

The scale and power of the multiplier effect would weigh on the average Joe; the idea that a small incremental improvement in a process, or a buck or two saved here and there, might have profoundly positive consequences across societies, communities and families. Study after study shows that the poor, most especially poor women, are prodigiously efficient with limited resources; that they more than anyone know how to stretch a rand.

The libertarian podcast boets like to pooh-pooh this kind of thing. But social grants mean people are able to function in society, and are able to care adequately for their children, who may, in turn, not end up as costly wards of the state. They can care for themselves to a level where, given an opportunity, it is at least possible for them to contribute – to get to work clothed, fed and housed.

Social grants are the thread upon which the lives of so many of our citizens depend. And Dlamini was indifferent to the point of caricature. It was Dlamini's job to ensure the handover of Sassa payments was done by 31 March 2017. Let's leave the commentary to the Constitutional Court, which was forced to rule on a matter brought by the Black Sash NGO – note, please, not through any government process – a matter of weeks ahead of the catastrophe that would have befallen millions of South Africans. Criticising Dlamini's "extraordinary conduct" with regard to a previous order that she get her Sassa ducks in a row, the court said that there was "no indication on the papers that [the minister] showed any interest in Sassa's progress before October last year".

"Since April 2016 the responsible functionaries of Sassa have been aware that it could not comply with the undertaking to the Court that it would be able to pay social grants from 1 April 2017. The

Minister was apparently informed of this only in October 2016. There is no indication on the papers that she showed any interest in Sassa's progress in that regard before that. Despite warnings from counsel and CPS, neither Sassa nor the Minister took any steps to inform the Court of the problems they were experiencing. Nor did they see fit to approach the Court for authorisation to regularise or ameliorate the situation. When, eventually, Sassa brought an application on 28 February 2017 for authorisation, the Minister intervened and ordered Sassa to withdraw the application. On 3 March 2017, the Minister and Sassa filed a supplementary progress report, without any acknowledgement that they were under any legal obligation to do so."

In the end, despite Dlamini's worst efforts, the crisis was averted. But it had been officially established that she didn't give a damn. As explained by constitutional legal whizz Pierre de Vos, "The people of South Africa (and the court) could not trust the South African Social Security Agency and Dlamini to do their job to ensure the delivery of social grants as required by the Constitution." She "could not be trusted not to mislead the Constitutional Court in future". In 2018, that's exactly what the court would find.

Throughout this sorry saga, Dlamini neglected her duty to such an extent that she has earned the ironic reputation as an enabler of what some might call white monopoly capital. In this instance, the company that benefited by repeated extensions to its contract was Cash Paymaster Services, which earned more than a billion rand's profits in the five years to 2017. The fellow who ran it in that time, Serge Belamant, survived various allegations that the company had used Black Economic Empowerment fronting to secure the original contract, and he received an estimated R263 million payout for his efforts on his resignation that year.

This should all be humiliating, career-ending stuff for the minister involved, right? Surprise! Of course not. Dlamini knew her real job was not the feeding of 12 million children; it was the backing of uBaba, her homie Jacob Zuma, at the upcoming ANC elective congress. Which, as

"The office which she occupied demands a greater commitment to ethical behaviour and requires a high commitment to public service. The Department of Social Development is as much responsible for the realisation of rights outlined in the Constitution as this court, and she used her position as minister of the department to place herself between constitutionally enshrined rights and those entitled to them...

"It has been a sorry saga, and it is proper that Minister Dlamini must, in her personal capacity, bear a portion of the costs. It would account for her degree of culpability in misleading the court, conduct which is deserving of censure by this court as a mark of displeasure, more so since she held a position of responsibility as a member of the Executive. Her conduct is inimical to the values underpinning the Constitution that she undertook to uphold when she took up office."

Constitutional Court ruling finding that Bathabile Dlamini had misled the court, September 2018

leader of the ANC Women's League, she did by bravely supporting JZ's anointed candidate, Nkosazana Dlamini-Zuma. Ultimately it was *that* that was her undoing. When Cyril Ramaphosa, no doubt to her surprise, won the presidency instead, she was removed, within two weeks, from the Social Development ministry and tucked away for safekeeping as the Minister of Women in the Presidency.

It was a necessary demotion, before her outright ejection from Cabinet in 2019, and yet there was some pathos in her relocation to a ministry that ostensibly oversees the wellbeing of South Africa's women. In a country that recorded 450,000 rape complaints in the decade to September 2019, and yet where the overwhelming majority of rapes go unreported, one cannot imagine a worse candidate to address yet another awful facet of South African life – not merely an indifferent placeholder, but someone who, as head cheerleader at the ANCWL, saw fit to stand firmly behind such an antediluvian symbol of philandering and sexist patriarchy as Jacob Zuma for so many years.

Bathabile Dlamini has few redeeming qualities. She is short on struggle history compared to others here, and there's no real contribution to anything other than the coffers of the Radisson Blu and the cellars of KWV. No innovation, no accomplishment that earns her a mitigating paragraph in our quest for fairness and balance, no small intervention that made something just a little bit better for millions in desperate need of the dignity that is their right.

Well, there is one thing.

She did manage to capture, in one short sentence, the depraved logic that has underpinned so much governmental wrongdoing throughout our lost decade. Her profound insight, the brief Eureka moment on which she rose as an Archimedean ringer of truth, her single instance of competence, was a phrase that explained how the edifice of Zuma Years state capture was not merely built on a foundation of quicksand, but that buried within were the skeletons of all who now walked the corridors of power and ran deals in its side rooms. And that uBaba knew precisely where they all lay.

"All of us there in the NEC," she said, speaking about the ANC's National Executive Committee, in an interview with the SABC in 2016, "have our smallanyana skeletons, and we don't want to take out all the skeletons because all hell will break loose."

And there you have it. Thank you, minister.

Before and since, however, nothing.

May her contribution to the misery of South Africa's poor, and her astounding indifference to them, never be forgotten.

Nkosazana Dlamini-Zuma

b. 27 January 1949

Minister of Cooperative Governance and Traditional Affairs; Minister in the Presidency (2018-2019); Minister of Home Affairs (2009-2012); Minister of Foreign Affairs (1999-2009); Minister of Health (1994-1999); Chairperson of the African Union Commission (2012-2017); JZ's ex; authoritarian vision of the hellscape alternative future we missed out on

IF THE COVID-19 LOCKDOWN CRISIS DID ANYTHING, it gave us a view of what life would have been like under President Nkosazana Dlamini-Zuma. In full cognisance of President Ramaphosa's twilight nightmare that he calls the "new dawn", we gained some real understanding of the calibre of the bullet we have dodged. Because for a while there she was pretty much our prime minister.

Despite her colourful attire and jaunty abbreviation, NDZ presents herself like the embodiment of Soviet architecture. Concrete, technocratic and unsmiling, she serves the coffee cold.

Dlamini-Zuma has been a permanent feature of our politics since democracy. Entire human beings have been born, educated and despatched into adult life during her tenure in high office. They turn 30 in three years. So experience on the job certainly isn't the issue here, although her track record is, despite what the strategically placed publicists will have had you believe over the years, a patchwork of mediocrity, fleeting competence and occasional disaster.

The traumatic flashbacks to her greatest hits were brought on by her overseeing, as head of Cooperative Governance, the handling of the Covid crisis. It was a nasty little hospital pass from Ramaphosa that would have been difficult to handle for the nimblest of political operators. And nimble NDZ is not, so it just brought out her authoritarian worst. Whatever faint vestiges of fun and lightness of being the global pandemic had allowed to remain by that point were systematically eradicated under her watchful eye. There would be no alcohol, no tobacco, certainly no zolling, and apparently no laughter or human warmth if she could help it.

In our quest to allocate praise where it is due, however, we must acknowledge Dlamini-Zuma's many years in exile. Also, she rescued Home Affairs from the bedlam that preceded her reign there from 2009. If you can remember a time when there was a competent Home Affairs department, then you remember the impact of Dlamini-Zuma.

Older readers, however, will further remember the scandal and nepotism that marked her initial role in Cabinet as Minister of Health going back to the Mandela presidency – a time in which the battle against Aids was marked by Virodene quackery and the *Sarafina II* "educational play" embarrassment (in hindsight, such a little cutie of a jobs-for-pals affair). And who can forget her tenure as foreign minister, around the turn of the century, when she looked on approvingly as Robert Mugabe turned the wonderful and functioning democracy north of our border to ruin? Presumably Minister Lindiwe Zulu, who in 2019 lamented the "millions of Zimbabweans living in South Africa" before exhorting them to get "involved in the resolution of the conflict in Zimbabwe". To remind her, they are here as a direct result of Dlamini-Zuma's "quiet diplomacy", which applauded Mugabe's narrow racial retribution at all costs while also happening to trash South Africa's newly earned moral standing in the international community.

And so to more recent times.

Jacob Zuma – NDZ's ex, if you hadn't worked it out, and much discussed elsewhere in this book – is forever mischaracterised. He is a traditional rural man of limited education. He doesn't understand money or business or economics or finance. That's all white monopoly capital to him. And yet he is notoriously charming and funny and, more than anything, is a genuinely gifted securocrat and ruthless politician. That's why, when it started to occur to him that he would not be president for life and that his successors, and their prosecutors, might have opinions on his laissez-faire attitude to the keys to our treasury, he set in motion a plan for his succession. To avoid the bad smell of local politics and ANC factionalism, he sent Nkosazana off to another exile, this time in Addis Ababa. There, amid some pushback, she managed to get herself elected as chair of the African Union. The initial difficulty was that it broke the unwritten rule that the larger economies do not put up candidates for the position, and the machinations required to

"A recent study by a reputable research institute compared the number of times [Nkosazana Dlamini-Zuma] smiled with the number of times former ANC spokesperson Carl Niehaus told the truth. The research, soon to be published in an academic journal, found that Niehaus told the truth more often than Dlamini-Zuma smiled."

Mondli Makhanya, May 2020

get her into it cemented South Africa's reputation on the continent as a bunch of arrogant wankers. But to hell with that, because for Zuma this was actually important – for his future freedom, he would need to parachute in a (relatively) untainted puppet candidate for election to the ANC presidency when his time was up.

And how very, very nearly it worked. *(See David Mabuza.)*

It is testament to the amount of damage inflicted on Zuma's watch that, three years after his failure to install his ex-wife and proxy candidate, we're in a hole as deep and dire as we are.

And as for Nkosazana Dlamini-Zuma, she was, we can only assume, happy to play the puppet and keep on digging. No smiley face for her.

Jack Dorsey

b. 19 November 1976

*Founder and CEO of Twitter; founder and CEO of Square;
righteous startup billionaire who thinks he can do
two things at once, but is doing such a bad job of
the first thing that it's actually ruining the world,
South Africa in particular*

Dishonourable mention: Mark Zuckerberg

IT'S TAKEN RATHER A WHILE, but the world is finally waking up to the realisation that social media isn't the fun little friend-making pastime it was made out to be way back in the mid-2000s, when it all seemed so new and exciting. Back then Tiger Woods was just a good golfer, Charlie Sheen was still on *Two And A Half Men*, and MySpace and its fresh competition, Facebook, were pioneering the Web 2.0. What could possibly go wrong?

Well, if you were MySpace, you could be consigned to the dustbin of internet history* by a brilliant young sociopath from Harvard; and if you were the human race, you could be duped into believing that nice progressive tech people in Silicon Valley were happy to give everyone in the world some harmless fun for free. Turns out they weren't. They were lining us up to sell our souls for filthy lucre.

Since those innocent newsfeed-free, likes-free, teenage-suicide-free days, social media has revealed itself for what it is: a modern psychology experiment being performed on billions of people around the world, based on the worst principles of growth-for-growth's-sake profiteering. And with the experiment results now coming in thick and fast, we're realising what's been foisted upon us. Social media makes us sad, envious and depressed; encourages bullying, victimisation and shaming; distracts us from doing meaningful things like working, relaxing or interacting with three-dimensional people face to face; reduces our ability to empathise with others; compartmentalises us and entrenches our biases; foments polarisation, intolerance and societal division; casts doubt on simple truth; and ultimately has a material effect on politics, elections and thus the healthy functioning of society.

If this is news to you, we suggest you put this book down right now and go watch *The Social Dilemma*. Not that people haven't been pointing this stuff out for years, but when the guy who co-invented the "like" button tells you it has the same effect on your dopamine levels as nicotine or crack cocaine, and the guy who "monetised" Facebook tells you his children are not allowed screen time, let alone social media time, it feels that much more real.

In short, they couldn't have invented a narcotic to do more damage than social media, which by now should really be called anti-society media. To do what they've done they had to create a digital drug, and then employ the world's finest Ivy League-trained engineers and most sophisticated AI to continuously refine it, year in and year out, to be

---

* Technically MySpace is still a thing.

more and more "habit-forming". As the historian Yuval Noah Harari has been warning for some time, the algorithms that control your social media feeds are designed to get to know you better than you know yourself. Why? So they can hack you.

They do this by using every super-refined psychological trick in the book to keep you "engaged" – that is, online on their platform, continually clicking, scrolling, watching – and then gathering as much data about you as possible in the process. What articles you read, what videos you watch, what links you chase, what posts you like, the number of milliseconds your mouse hovers over a particular image.

All this effort is so they can sell you to advertisers for targeted marketing, which they do in spades. This is the essence of "surveillance capitalism", and in itself it isn't necessarily the end of the world. Most of us don't actually mind good, relevant advertising, and it's possibly one of the reasons why people struggle to see the enormous net negative that social media presents to society. If we're now seeing ads that are more relevant to us – fewer Tampax ads if that's not your thing, fewer *Call of Duty* ads if you're not a gamer – then isn't that a good idea?

The problem comes in the collateral damage of keeping us engaged. And, if we haven't made it clear enough, the damage is monstrous. It is cluster bombs over the very fabric of civilised society and depleted uranium left in the water that irrigates our daily conversation. When sensible political commentators such as Douglas Murray and Richard Kreitner speak of "the possible dissolution of the United States" or even the threat of a second civil war, this is only because anti-social media has made this possible.

In the US, Mark Zuckerberg is rightly the prime target for opprobrium when this topic is raised. There are many reasons why he has in recent years been called to defend Facebook before Congress, and why he's the first name on the list when MSNBC host Joe Scarborough writes, "Mark, Sheryl and Jack, you have revealed yourselves to be vapid vulgarians who put at risk Americans' health, racial justice, fair elections and basic truths."

One is that Facebook's own research found, in 2018, that their "algorithms exploit the human brain's attraction to divisiveness" and that, without intervention, they would feed users "more and more divisive content in an effort to gain user attention and increase time on the platform". (Facebook shelved the report.) Another is that foreign influence over Facebook groups had a material effect on the US elections in 2016.

Facebook is the world's biggest social media platform, with around 2.7 billion unique monthly users; it owns the third-, fourth- and sixth-biggest social networks*; and Zuckerberg isn't just CEO, he's the majority shareholder. What he says goes, which makes him quite probably the most influential individual in the world. All of which makes his ongoing refusal to act decisively against the damage his platforms are doing to societies everywhere that much more unforgivable.

If US antitrust hearings don't result in Facebook being broken up, the US really is doomed. But as much as we have argued that Zuckerberg is the modern world's Antichrist *(see 50 People Who Stuffed Up The World)*, his influence in South Africa is outdone by another smug punch-me-in-the-face tech geek who refuses to make the connection between the destructive results of his particular social network and how he runs it.

This is hipster-bearded Jack Dorsey, the third of Scarborough's vulgarians (the other being Sheryl Sandberg of Facebook), and co-

---

* Respectively, WhatsApp (about two billion unique users), Facebook Messenger (1.3 billion) and Instagram (1.1 billion).

founder and current CEO of Twitter. Though Twitter has a reported ad reach of 2.3 million users in South Africa compared to 20 million on Facebook, it is the social network that has powered much of our racialised online rage and declining journalistic standards over the last decade. Not just that; it made a specific and material contribution to the Guptas' state capture operation that caused so much harm to our politics, economy and society. *(See Victoria Geoghegan.)* For allowing this damage, Dorsey gets our big thumbs down ahead of the Zuck.

In South Africa, our elections are not (yet) targeted for manipulation via Facebook sites. Rather, our entire political landscape is targeted for manipulation by Twitter bots, trolls, sock puppets and bad actors. And Twitter is used as a bullhorn to initiate real physical and economic damage, as when Julius Malema tweeted, on 6 September 2020: "@Clicks_SA see you tomorrow. Fellow fighters and ground forces; ATTACK!!!" This was in response to a thoughtless Clicks advertisement for TRESemmé shampoo, which the ever-alert Malema used to generate headlines and relevance for his party. The following day, 7 September, several Clicks stores were vandalised by EFF members and dozens forced to close. On 8 September, Clicks chose to shutter 400 stores to avert further mayhem. Thousands of mostly black staff were affected.

With a single tweet Malema had managed to mobilise an army of chaos and amplify a racially insensitive incident into a racial war. The most telling vignette caught on camera was a white "granny" pulling a gun on black EFF supporters outside a Clicks store at the Walmer Park Shopping Centre in Port Elizabeth. The woman and several EFF members were arrested.

Thus we see the cause-and-effect processes of Twitter. Emotions triggered. Biases entrenched. Rage and conflict exploding online and ultimately in reality. This would be terrible in any society, but in one with such a history of division as ours it is devastating. South Africa is a society desperate for healing, for bridging the gaps between races and classes; and this requires human interaction and empathy – both of which are entirely eliminated on Twitter because of its complete lack of shared reality. Instead, we have egomaniacs and narcissists, who

> "For the good of their profession, their mental health, and indeed wider society, they [journalists] should all get off Twitter now. And they should never, ever come back."
>
> *Thomas Moller-Nielsen*

in no way represent the average South African, supposedly leading the national narrative, aided and abetted by lowlife politicians who know the value of race-war distractions, and an underfunded and poorly led media.

Which brings us to the next point: how our journalists have fallen so hard for it.

A quarter of Twitter's authenticated worldwide users are journalists or media organisations, but as philosopher Thomas Moller-Nielsen explains it, if you were to design a platform to actively reduce journalistic standards at global scale, you would be hard-pressed to do better than inventing Twitter. While offering "a veneer of journalistic utility", it remains "strictly at odds with the aims of the journalism profession". As a social network, one of its inherent abilities is to customise its user experience and so keep people in their echo chambers, isolated from an objective view of the world. And Twitter, specifically, is a killer of objective truth – a 2018 MIT study showed that fake news on Twitter spreads six times faster than real news. It is also entirely unrepresentative of the public at large. Twitter fights and toxic meltdowns are the equivalent of deranged soapbox evangelists going at each other after a bender, and really do not merit being turned into supposed news articles.

If the inability to disseminate objective and meaningful truth to the public is the death of journalism, here's the nail in the coffin: Twitter (along with Facebook) steals the precious advertising revenue that might otherwise have gone to actual media companies so desperate for it.

When does journalistic self-awareness alight on the realisation that spending more time on Twitter than doing actual journalism is self-defeating and ruinous? Perhaps that time is nigh.

Twitter came into being in 2006, but its rise in South Africa matches remarkably closely the period covered in this book. We might, for practical purposes, say that Twitter has had a valid political presence here since Mandy Wiener and colleagues started live-tweeting the Jackie Selebi corruption trial in April 2010. It's been downhill ever since.

In July 2020 the editor of *News24*, Adriaan Basson, who had tweeted alongside Wiener at the trial, announced he was stepping back from Twitter. "Almost exactly ten years ago, I was one of the first South African journalists to join Twitter," he wrote. "The biggest mistake the media made was to think Twitter is representative of the reading population or the public at large; that journalists should go to Twitter to know what South Africans say and think."

Well, yes. And what a pity so few journalists have done likewise.

How is it that supposedly savvy newsroom editors and online media operators have been so blind to the damage it causes? Do they really not see it, or are they so desperate for the clicks to pay the bills that they feel it's the moral price they have to pay to do real journalism?

What a slippery ethical slope that is – not too far removed from the practices of the dodgy politicians and businessmen that those real journalists investigate.

Social media platforms in their current format epitomise broken capitalism. They prioritise shareholders with absolute disregard for the commonwealth. They promote hatred, division and radicalisation, and Twitter – with far fewer users than Facebook, YouTube, Instagram or even TikTok – is optimised for this in particular. But Dorsey appears to have no idea of the damage it does. If he did, he wouldn't spend half his time working at another company; he is CEO of both Twitter and the financial payments company Square. He wouldn't announce he was going to spend a year swanning about Africa rather than knuckling down at HQ to resolve real issues that affect hundreds of millions of real people. (His plans were put on hold by Covid-19.) He wouldn't claim that Twitter's "purpose is to serve the public conversation", which is quite evidently the polar opposite of what it does.

If we were to summarise him in a couple of tweets, Dorsey is an ice-bathing, silent-retreating, righteous asshole who on one hand can preach about "social justice reform" and donate $10 million to Ibram X Kendi's Center for Antiracist Research to promote "equity and justice for all", and on the other hand lacks the self-awareness to realise that the company he leads is actively sickening the world, not healing it. Or, perhaps, he "just, simply put, doesn't give a shit", in the words of tech commentator Scott Galloway, and is also a member of the Silicon Valley sociopath club.

Either way, there is a raft of rather easy fixes for Twitter: first one, get a new CEO.

One of the devil's greatest tricks, as Keyser Söze knew so well, was to make you think he doesn't exist. In that sense Twitter is the darkest of angels. Its hundreds of millions of users clearly have no idea how it's addling their minds; our news editors and journalists are only now catching on to the damage it causes; and its part-time CEO Jack Dorsey appears to be, like Del Amitri, the last to know.

Rage may be its speciality, but rage isn't exclusive to Twitter: #screwyoujack.

See Adri Senekal de Wet.

Jessie Duarte & Gwede Mantashe

Duarte: b. 19 September 1953
Mantashe: b. 21 June 1955

*Deputy Secretary General (since 2012) and Secretary
General (2007-2017) of the ANC; high priests of the broad
church of ANC contradiction; defenders of the ANC faith
and enablers of its unaccountability*

LET US BEGIN THIS FIRST OF SEVERAL ENTRIES in the book on the
structural problems that define the ruling party of South Africa with a
"who said it?" humdinger. Which of these quotes is from George Orwell
and which is from an ANC elder and ex-president of South Africa?

"The leaders will now enjoy the champagne, and of course they do so on your behalf through their lips."

"Day and night we are watching over your welfare. It is for *your* sake that we drink that milk and eat those apples."

The apples and milk do rather give the game away – that's from *Animal Farm*, of course, published in 1945. But how is that first quote *not* Orwell? How is it not an unlikely parody of the worst of authoritarian propaganda?

Tragically, it isn't. It is from the mouth of Kgalema Motlanthe, no less, delivered in earnest at the ANC's 100-year celebration to a crowd of restive proletariat in the Free State Stadium in Bloemfontein in January 2012.

It was Orwell's genius to reveal the machinations of totalitarian corruption to the world in allegory form that even children could understand; more so that he's still getting it right so many decades later. And to see just how right, let's play out the full milk and apple quote, uttered in the book by the fat little pig known as Squealer.

"Day and night we are watching over your welfare. It is for *your* sake that we drink that milk and eat those apples. Do you know what would happen if we pigs failed in our duty? Jones would come back! Yes, Jones would come back! Surely, comrades, surely there is no-one among you who wants to see Jones come back?"

There it is: the Orwellian insight into how a senior ANC official might get away with a line of such callous disregard with barely a raised eyebrow, and indeed how the ANC has survived so long in power despite doing such a disastrous job of governing the country. The fear of "Jones" is an essential tenet of ANC dogma.

In the book, Squealer is second in command on Manor Farm and head of propaganda, a position largely paralleled in our little comparison here with that of Secretary-General of the ANC, effectively the party CEO, who throughout the Zuma Years was Gwede Mantashe.

The problem of who is in charge at the ANC has been, since the party's national conference at Nasrec in December 2017, pronounced, to say the least. It is the focus of the party's factionalism, and to many it is the very battle of good versus evil in modern South Africa. We will come, in future pages, to how Ace Magashule came to occupy the position of SG of the ANC, and the uncertainty and damage he causes there. But before we get there we must give space to his forerunner, Gwede Mantashe, and his (and Ace's) deputy, Jessie Duarte. Because, make no mistake, when Mantashe was SG of the ANC, he was in charge. So much so that he was generally accepted to be the second-most-powerful person in the country. He was Zuma's enforcer – and Duarte became the enforcer's enforcer.

It has become a useful cliché to describe the ANC as "a broad church". It really is filled with capitalists and communists, free marketeers and statists, BEE fat cats and Marxist trade unionists, real struggle veterans and less real struggle veterans – "a strange combination of highly acquisitive behaviour and socialist ideology", as one commentator put it. And it is the ongoing role of the SG and his deputy to serve the varied congregation faithfully so that they might be at peace with their individual places in the universe.

Mantashe and Duarte showed constant devotion to the cause under Zuma, even as its contradictions were rattling its foundations. They were the ones who stood in front of the cameras – now with an SACP cap on (Mantashe was its chair for six years), now wearing Cartier shades – fighting the good fight, declaring miracles, banishing unholy thoughts.

The fundamental contradiction for them to square was how the party of the people could allow so many of its members to become obscenely wealthy – both legally, through economic policies that exacerbate inequality, and illegally, through gross corruption – at the cost of those who are poor. How it could "ensure that South Africa does belong to all who live in it", in Duarte's own words, but sell it out to a family of swindlers from abroad. One imagines them spending hours praying hard over that last one, especially around 2016, as the Gupta house of cards started to collapse.

Back then, Mantashe and Duarte had spearheaded a move by the ANC and its Cabinet members to bring pressure to bear on the big four South African banks for being part of "white monopoly capital oppressing black-owned businesses". Why? Because they had dared to close the accounts of Oakbay Investments, the Gupta family's holding company, through which it ran the bulk of its state capture operation. The ANC approach followed a direct request from Oakbay.

In 2018 (as deputy to Magashule), Duarte went on record to defend the party's decision to appoint Tony Yengeni to chair its crime and corruption committee. Yengeni, famously, is the only politician who has served prison time for Arms Deal corruption, having failed to declare a discount he had received on a Mercedes-Benz. "The conviction of comrade Tony Yengeni worries many in the ANC," said Duarte. "What are we saying? If you negotiate a vehicle in this country you dare not negotiate a discount because that's corruption?"

It's important to understand that both Mantashe and Duarte are intelligent and streetwise. Whereas it can serve the party's purposes to allow a few dummies in Cabinet – to say thank you for their service to the cause, or because it's useful to have a few pliable morons in positions of power – smarts are an absolute requirement for the SG positions. Mantashe honed his skills over many years at the National Union of Mineworkers and as a Boksburg councillor. Duarte, in turn, learnt at the foot of Mandela himself, first as his assistant, and later as the spokeswoman for the ANC. These are not positions for the weak of spirit or mind.

"In recent years, especially since the infamous Polokwane conference, we have observed so much ill-discipline from ANC members, and yet few remedial or corrective actions are taken. This is not only worrisome but blatantly disgusting, because it presupposes that no-one in the ANC sees anything wrong with the conduct of certain members."
Oscar van Heerden, author and ANC member

Yet it appears that even the sharpest minds can fall victim to the self-deception of faith and thus enable truly abominable behaviour. Author Michael Shermer might have been speaking of Duarte and Mantashe when he noted that, "Smart people believe weird things because they are skilled at defending beliefs they arrived at for non-smart reasons."

Mantashe was the man who orchestrated Zuma's rise to the top at Polokwane, came to form a partnership with him of unprecedented power, and then for so long offered his wiles and savvy in the defence of a man who was so clearly doing structural and reputational damage to South Africa. In the same way, Duarte became the apostolic guard who defended every bridge a cadre might walk over to deliver his or her gift of patronage. You could even be a convicted criminal, as with Yengeni, and she would defend you just as long as you wore an ANC T-shirt.

The contradictions at the heart of the battle between party and state were well illustrated in Mantashe's attitude to Public Protector Thuli Madonsela, once she began, in 2012, to investigate the misuse of state funds for upgrades to Zuma's Nkandla homestead in KwaZulu-Natal. In response, Mantashe was at the forefront of an aggressive and personal ANC response that would come to symbolise the party's wretched willingness to defend the indefensible.

Yet at the farewell dinner to honour her departure from office in 2016, Mantashe then said, "I agree with Premier David Makhura when he said you saved us from ourselves. You did and we never acknowledged that. You leave the ANC wiser as you go."

So which is it? Was she "playing tactics", "protecting the interests of a particular section of society", consistently trying to "discredit the ANC and its leadership in government"? Or was she saving it?

Existential questions for the high priests of the ANC, you might think. Except no. Because even today, with Zuma gone, you suspect that Mantashe and Duarte adhere to neither side of that particular dilemma. They were just doing what needed to be done at the time, because the real dogma for them – the unwritten scripture that defined their roles – was simply that the party must be protected, in the moment, at all costs. Never mind what happened yesterday or what may happen tomorrow.

> "How long will you defend the unjust and show partiality to the wicked?
>
> Defend the cause of the weak and fatherless, maintain the rights of the poor and oppressed.
>
> Rescue the weak and needy, deliver them from the hand of the wicked.
>
> They know nothing, they understand nothing.
>
> They walk about in darkness; all the foundations of the earth are shaken."
>
> *Psalm 82*

Remember that while Mantashe supported him, Zuma remained in power. Without Mantashe, Zuma could not survive. They say the turning point was Nenegate. *(See Des van Rooyen.)* Wherever it may have been, it raises the question: did Mantashe eventually abandon Zuma because finally, after all these years, his eyes were suddenly opened to the destruction of the state capture project undertaken on his watch? Or was he simply following his faith? A faith in the ANC above all else that is unshakeable across so much of the party, and thus explains so much of the tragedy of the last decade?

See David Mabuza, Ace Magashule, Supra Mahumapelo, Baleka Mbete, Gavin Watson.

The fund manager

Not particularly effective investor of money; always
incomprehensible, often unnecessary drain on the pockets
and pensions of many South Africans

A POINT WORTH MAKING IN THESE ORWELLIAN TIMES is that, despite the familiar Siberian chill of expropriative glee that gusts through the commentary of the comfortable, wealth is no crime.

Equally, setting out to impoverish those who have attained it does nothing to advance and dignify those who have not. This is not some verisimilar idea, but is as true and as immovable as the koppies of the Great Karoo.

In fact, persistent and endemic poverty is of far greater concern than the far lower incidence of prodigious wealth. It should be what exercises us and tugs at our conscience more than anything. It is regrettably easy to simply blame the rich, and so it remains a dispiritingly successful and long-lived deceit that poverty is created by the wealthy.

In any case, if for the purposes of this entry we can agree that wealth is not a crime in itself, then it must be something else that catapults our poor fund manager onto our list. We know that he, unlike so many others between these covers, probably did not steal a cent, and indeed that he didn't need to bother.

The fund manager finds himself here because he is a talisman for an industry that has given customers sub-inflation returns and consistently underperformed the indices during this miserable last decade. In this time of political chaos, when some financial stability might have helped us sleep a smidgen better at night, he delivered worse-than-mediocre work while he and his brethren continued to remunerate themselves stratospherically and, in another unforgivable crime, build vast swathes of Higgovale while they were at it.

South African fund managers, also known as asset managers (same difference, if you didn't know), tend to live in different cities to our wanker bankers, though they traverse similar ethical terrain. The former congregate on the mountain slopes of Cape Town, while the latter can be found cruising around Westcliff and Saxonwold in Johannesburg. The former, as a rule of thumb, wangle their money from the financially illiterate; the latter do their wangling from the financially literate. If you need an example, a fund manager might, via his army of financial advisers, convince a working-class stiff to invest his pension in a money-sink the workings of which he cannot comprehend, while a wanker banker might convince a corporate CEO to buy a down-and-out retailer in Australia that then loses said corporate billions over the next five years and costs the CEO his job.

With the definitions established, let us get past another notion here. Whingeing about wanker bankers might be a game for the wealthy, but complaining about fund managers absolutely is not. What they do affects anyone with a pension, whether they mop the floor or own the company. Getting it right really matters, especially in South Africa, where people don't save enough for retirement and are cast onto the mortuary slab of state services or become a burden to their family once they stop working.

And so let us deal with a remarkable statistic. Over the years 2014-2019 three out of four South African fund managers underperformed the market, according to the S&P Indices versus Active (SPIVA) South Africa scorecard. Instead they fiddled, using their enormously expensive insight to actively manage portfolios of investments, with the end result being that the people whose money they were playing with were made poorer in real terms, and sometimes even in actual terms. For this service they charged a whopping 3%, which they spent on plastering Higgovale with festering carbuncles and hindering the movement of the productive workforce on their R200,000 bicycles. This is why, if you speak to any vaguely competent financial advisers, they will laugh – a-ha-ha-ha – at the positively hilarious industry understanding that the bulk of fund managers are likely to lose you money.

One riposte from the managers' camp is that it's unfair to judge them in a bull market, and that their clients will be grateful when the markets start tanking. But when exactly that happened in early 2020, with great big piles of Covid poo in extreme motion, it turned out they were too busy improving their PBs for the Cycle Tour to notice.

The failure of the fund-management industry presents a difficult challenge. It obviously cannot be regulated by the state (let's not give the comrades any bright ideas), but it also seems incapable of self-regulating, of finding a way to align how it remunerates itself with the returns it gives its customers.

> "[A]ctive managers who aim to beat the market by picking winning stocks have long predicted that demand for their expertise would return if conditions become more volatile, and the time for that revelation would seem to be upon us. Global stocks crashed as the Covid-19 pandemic ripped around the world, and the most common measure of volatility, the VIX, reached a historic peak. But the active managers' supposed return to glory was underwhelming at best."
>
> *Ruan Jooste, April 2020*

For most clients, fund managers have become destroyers of wealth, an active drain on prosperity – and the opacity of what these people do is key to the mugging-in-motion they represent. The industry's language is clannish and exclusionary. The "product portfolios" the firms offer are as baffling to decode as an Enigma machine or your Vodacom contract. Nobody has time for it and we just let the professionals get on with it. It is an industry that thrives on its own clients' confusion and intimidation, the fact that we're all too embarrassed to say to some slimeball in ostentatious Italian shoes that "I have no clue what all this means, and it is a legal requirement that falls on you, not me, to get me to understand it, so start speaking in plain English, pal…"

One day you'll need your pension, either way. And if you were to work out where your money's gone, the chances are more than likely that you'll discover that the fees you've paid to your fund-management firm are eye-wateringly close to equalling the gains you've made on your portfolio, which, as we've mentioned, will be worse than the broader index in three out of four cases.

It's at this point you may ask, "Where the hell is my money?" The answer is made of carbon fibre and resides between your fund manager's sweaty balls, a toy that he parks in the fifth garage at *Maison Travertine* in Higgovale. And yes, you paid for that too, along with the Porsche Cayenne that the trophy wife uses to take Hugo to Bishops every morning.

To steal a Wall Street anecdote and ham-fistedly mash it onto Cape Town, is it not reasonable to ask where the bulk of the clients' houses are? They're in Goodwood and Pimville and Mamelodi and Melville and Durban North, that's where. These are the neighbourhoods where people who create wealth and add value to the economy live.

When did you last speak to the people looking after your pension? Perhaps consider doing just that, finding out how much you've paid them, and how much value they've delivered for that fee. The chances are it'll blow your socks off.

The fund manager is a tick on the ballsack of the working South African. It's time he explained – in English – what the hell it is he actually does for us.

Victoria Geoghegan

b. 27 June 1983

*Mind polluter; Gupta reputation launderer; architect of
the destructive, racially divisive campaign to sustain state
capture; cause of Bell Pottinger's self-destruction; poster girl
for amoral psycho-corporate public relations that sees no
qualms in the destabilisation of entire countries*

*Dishonourable mentions: Timothy Bell, the Guptas,
James Henderson, Mzwanele Manyi, Andile Mngxitama*

ONCE UPON A TIME, VICTORIA GEOGHEGAN was an ambitious upper-
level executive on a straight-line trajectory to the top of the public-
relations universe. Now she is the face of the dramatic implosion of one

of the world's most recognisable and influential PR companies, and an unholy symbol of the public's almost complete mistrust in the industry she represents. Also, everyone in South Africa hates her.

The PR company that Geoghegan once worked for, and once existed, was Bell Pottinger, a UK-based operation with a reputation for embracing the seediest of well-paying clients, from Oscar Pistorius and Rolf Harris to the Pinochet Foundation and the wife of Bashar al-Assad. Its confidential client list was, one imagines, a stolen photocopy of the Devil's Rolodex.

In 2016, Bell Pottinger took on one client too many, however: the Gupta brothers, friends of President Zuma of South Africa and his immediate family. The full extent of that relationship was being incrementally revealed in the South African and international press at the time, with undesirable results for the brothers and their businesses. They were being painted as criminals and corrupters who influenced the highest political decisions in the land, plundered the South African treasury and economy at will, and really belonged in jail. The court of public opinion was becoming increasingly hostile, equating Zuma and the Guptas with the new concept of state capture, and important banks and financial institutions were refusing to do business with them. The "Zuptas" needed a PR makeover – or, at least, something to distract their critics from their shameless appropriation of state resources.

Enter Bell Pottinger, apparently introduced to the Guptas by two men intimately involved in the global arms trade: Fana Hlongwane, notorious for his role in South Africa's corrupt and wasteful Arms Deal, and Christopher Geoghegan, former COO of BAE Systems, which was one of the chief beneficiaries of said deal and also a Bell Pottinger client. Fast-forward through the relevant meetings and strategy discussions and a fee agreement of £100,000 per month plus expenses, and Geoghegan's daughter Victoria found herself heading up the account of Oakbay Investments, the Guptas' holding company. All very cosy to this point.

Having joined Bell Pottinger at age 21, Victoria Geoghegan apparently had no qualms about dealing with the odd ropey client – with her father happy to sell overpriced fighter trainers to the South African government, sleeping peacefully after a hard day's unconscionable work presumably runs in the family. Rather, she took a fast route up the career ladder, and under her guidance Bell Pottinger orchestrated the dissemination of a new narrative for the South African public to consume: the hoodoo of "white monopoly capital".

Essentially a childlike no-*you*-are! response to the criticisms of state capture, claims of white monopoly capital dumped the blame for South Africa's increasingly dire economic situation into the laps of white-owned businesses that were supposedly still running the country and reaping the spoils of apartheid. The briefest moment of lucid thought on the matter would reveal what bunk this idea was, but the ambitious and apparently amoral Geoghegan knew, as any vaguely competent PR minion does, that it's hearts, not minds, that matter in such campaigns. Led by an army of fake Twitter accounts – Twitterbots – the message went out: *It's all about race.* This is a powerful method of distraction just about anywhere in the world these days, but in South Africa, a country defined by its history of racial division, this was as cynical and reprehensible a move as could be imagined. It was a campaign that would later be described by the UK's Public Relations and Communications Association (PRCA), the largest PR association in Europe, as "by any reasonable standard of judgment likely to inflame racial discord", "beyond the pale" and "the most serious breach of our code of conduct in the history of the organisation".

In this instance, however, it was also a campaign that was quite easily identified. The Twitterbots gave themselves away with a predilection for transmitting Gupta propaganda at exactly the same time, geolocators that revealed they were created in India, and laughably unlikely spreadsheet-generated names such as Bongi Vorster, Dlamini Louw and Iminathi Junior. There was a sense of shamelessness to it all that might fly in South Africa, where the Zuptas were so used to doing what they want and getting away with it, but once the UK press picked up on the story, Geoghegan, her campaign and Bell Pottinger itself were doomed. Major clients departed almost overnight, and the (non-Twitterbot) social-media response was vehement and determined. Geoghegan had committed the fatal PR crime of becoming the story and, with flaming irony, social-media rage would ensure she was fired for her efforts.

In December 2016, at the age of just 33, Victoria Geoghegan had been appointed MD of Bell Pottinger's financial and corporate division, reward for her work on the Gupta account. In July 2017, she was forced to resign, along with others who had worked with her. Two months later, Bell Pottinger was expelled from the PRCA for five years for inciting racial hatred, acting against the public interest and generally bringing the industry into disrepute. A week after that, the company went into administration.

It is worth pointing out that the destruction of Bell Pottinger was a rare instance in which mass social-media rage became a force for good. For those who might be tempted to overstate the case, however, let's not forget how it all began in the first place. Geoghegan had harnessed the destructive powers of social media, and her weapon of choice eventually backfired and sunk her.

No-one who knows the story is likely to take her for a good, decent human being. Over the course of a year or so, she became the demon in the average South African's ear, a disseminator of social poison who cared nought for the damage she was wreaking on an entire country – someone who proudly displayed her charitable credentials as a supporter of schoolchildren in Nigeria, while being intimately involved in undermining the future of schoolchildren in South Africa.

It must be acknowledged, though, that she was hardly acting in isolation, and two of the great modern PR sharks deserve special

"[The Guptas] looked at where we are fragile as a society. The first point where we are the most soft, the most fragile, is race relations... The easiest thing they've done is to resuscitate some of the terms that were there. Concepts such as 'white monopoly capital', 'radical economic transformation' – those terms were meant just to divide."
Ralph Mathekga, interviewed in the documentary Influence

mention whenever her name crops up. They are Timothy Bell and James Henderson.

As Margaret Thatcher's top spin doctor and then the founder of Bell Pottinger itself, the late Baron Bell was essentially British PR aristocracy, which may sound rather fancy but should not, we'd suggest, be considered an aspirational status unless being a self-inflated arse of dubious morality correlates with your vision of greatness. For an immediate sense of the man, we recommend watching the award-winning 2020 documentary *Influence*, of which he is the unapologetically frank focal point. Bell was intimately involved in, and excited by, the early negotiations with his company's new clients, the Guptas, but with the self-preservation instincts of a gutter weasel on garbage day, he soon spotted the impending disaster and skittered into disaffected and condescending exile in August 2016. When Tim Bell doesn't want your business, you know you're bad news.

Henderson, meanwhile, the CEO of Bell Pottinger with the oleaginous sheen of an otter in an oil slick, lacked such foresight. After pushing the *how-should-I-know-what-my-employees-were-up-to?* defence as far as it could go, he was forced to take a fall just days before the PRCA ruling in September 2017 – but his resignation proved futile. His fiancée Heather Kerzner, the socialite ex-wife of Sol Kerzner, had invested millions of pounds in Bell Pottinger only months before the Gupta scandal started playing out, and together the two owned 37% of the company, a share that quickly became worthless. A few days after Henderson's resignation, the Henderson-Kerzner wedding was put on indefinite hold. There's only so much schadenfreude to be extracted in the circumstances, but South African observers took what they could.

Bell, who died in 2019, and Henderson were industry heavyweights who had built up Bell Pottinger into an enormously effective multinational that employed hundreds of people and influenced millions in countries across the world, from Chile to Iraq. This was hardly a case in isolation, so it says rather a lot that what they allowed to happen in South Africa was so loathsome that it sunk their business.

> "Well, they said, 'We want to run a campaign [saying] that all the money is stuck with the white people and there's nothing left for you.' And we said, 'Look, I'm sure we can manage something. We can organise marches in the streets, demonstrations.'"
>
> *Tim Bell, interviewed in Influence*

Anyone with the vaguest understanding of human nature knows that deep in the heart of all people – less deep in some than in others – lie the calcified seams of our worst terrors and instincts: racism, bigotry, fear of the other. It's taken thousands of years of civilisation to temper these embers of potential destruction with mutual respect and understanding, and codified laws, so that we might get along and build societies together, and in so doing lift up all within them.

South Africa, with its particular past, will always be prone to those looking to stoke the embers to their own advantage, and mostly the attempts are raw, instinctive and inherently political. Mzwanele "Jimmy" Manyi – putting it out there, as Director-General of Labour in 2010, that there were too many coloureds in the Western Cape. The white genocide crowd – always gunning for its own purified and independent homeland. The EFF – practically founded on this way of being. Andile Mngxitama of Black First Land First – a guy so toxic even the EFF expelled him, and yet so incoherent in his thinking that he was happy to work with "capital" Bell Pottinger and consider them "friends".

But righteous, indignant and even understandable race-baiting, as destructive as it is, is somehow less repugnant than the weaponised, monetised programme of influence that Victoria Geoghegan put her name to on behalf of Bell Pottinger. She did her bit to tear apart a country without, it would appear, the merest scruple on her face, only the monthly retainer and her career trajectory in mind.

There are, sadly, rather a lot of Victoria Geoghegans in the PR industry, but she just happened to be the one who ignored every *single* moral fibre in her body. The one who seems to have done whatever her clients, the godawful Guptas, wanted done, even if it meant gilding the enormous turd they had dumped on South Africa and its people.

As of September 2020, Geoghegan and Henderson, along with a colleague named Nick Lambert, had been targeted for formal directorship disqualification by the Insolvency Service in the UK. The bare minimum, we'd say. Jail sentences would be more appropriate.

Malusi Gigaba

b. 30 August 1971

*Former minister of Public Enterprises, Home Affairs
and (can you believe it?!) Finance; once promising young
political gun; Zupta bagman; victim of his own ego
and vanity – and Zuma's sharp eye*

Dishonourable mentions: the Guptas, Jacob Zuma

SOUTH AFRICA'S MOST FAMOUS PENIS belongs to Malusi Gigaba. It was just a short video clip in the trainwreck-in-perpetuity that is Gigaba's personal life, but in suggesting that the viewer "imagine this was in your mouth" it struck a certain chord.

To be sure, it was a hard no from us, thanks – but then again, Gigaba was at pains to stress that the video was private and intended for his wife

Norma, not Pornhub, which is where it trended, and that he was aware that his phone was hacked on a regular basis and woe is he. Which raises the question: if you're a high-profile political figure and you know your phone is vulnerable, why on earth would you send dick pics?

This little vignette regarding Gigaba's inability to successfully manage his home affairs might in a sensible country have given his seniors pause for thought. Because it was hardly the first time Gigaba had let his vanity get the better of him. But here, where the president can be a philandering kleptocrat with the single-minded purpose to enable the sacking of public finances and institutions, "appropriate" means something completely different.

And so it came to pass that Malusi Gigaba became one of the Zuptas' go-to guys. This after it had all begun with so much promise.

Knowledge Malusi Nkanyezi Gigaba took a well-worn political journey from apartheid schooling in his native Zululand to university at Durban-Westville and then on to the Communist Party and the ANC. His obvious talents saw him elected Youth League president three times in a row. He seemed diligent and serious, and Thabo Mbeki saw enough in the man to appoint him to the position of deputy minister of Home Affairs in 2004 at the age of 32.

The defenestration of Mbeki by Zuma's thugs at the ANC National Conference in Polokwane in 2007 was a moment of moral inflection in our country, when those walking a certain path might be tempted to turn down another. When apparently good people might start doing noticeably bad things. When Zuma, the ultimate securocrat, might look to identify those he regarded as pliable, just as his managers, the Gupta brothers, had identified him.

People who run spies will tell you that they are less like Fleming's James Bond and more like Le Carré's George Smiley. They are not inevitable forces of nature; rather, their handlers have something on them. Or, as Bathabile Dlamini showed us in her lone moment of public insight, there are smallanyana skeletons to be used as leverage. But the leverage is not always dirt from the past. In some cases it is a vulnerability in the present, and there is no vulnerability in modern South Africa quite like, as Hansie Cronje once explained it, an "unfortunate love of money". So it would seem that the trappings of high office and obscene wealth appealed to Malusi Gigaba's sense of self-importance.

Once Zuma ascended to the presidency in 2009, it didn't take too long. He needed a bag boy at the department of Public Enterprises to allow the Guptas to get going with the looting of their choice of state-owned enterprises (SOEs), so in 2010 he fired the impeccably qualified lifelong ANC lefty Barbara Hogan, and appointed Gigaba. His principal qualification appeared to be averting his gaze.

Towards the end of his catastrophic reign at Public Enterprises, when the wrecking ball of state capture was bashing at the pillars of SAA, Transnet and Eskom, Gigaba appeared at the State of the Nation Address in an SAA pilot's uniform. To say this is inappropriate doesn't begin to express it. A340 and 747 captains need huge experience, and those who have flown for our national carrier are highly regarded. As SAA has now all but collapsed, its captains have become hot property on the global aviation market, and that very South African stab of pride-rage no doubt awaits us in the near future as we hear our Emirates Captain Willem van der Merwe welcome us on flight EK-what-what to Dubai. Which is to say that Gigaba doesn't have the right to appropriate the uniform of a cartoon character, let alone a South African Airways captain.

It would seem Gigaba's ongoing problem is "reading the room". The opening of Parliament is a grotesque circus in which our corrupt government officials flaunt what they've bought with the money they've stolen from us. It is not a nine-year-old's fancy-dress party.

Moving on to Home Affairs later in 2014, Gigaba became the poster boy for the destruction of tourism by implementing, doubling down on, changing and then giving up on the most absurd visa regulations in the world. They required that children coming into the country carry with them an unabridged birth certificate and a letter of consent from any non-present parent, and they proved enormously frustrating for tourists wanting to come and spend foreign currency in our country. How this benefited the Zupta cabal is not clear, and it's possible that it may have simply been to hurt the Western Cape which, with actual strategic intent, was successfully growing inbound tourist numbers year-on-year, but had a nasty habit of voting for the wrong people. Whatever the reason, it seems Gigaba's fragile ego played a part.

When Redi Tlhabi, respected author and radio personality, suggested on Twitter that the entire visa shambles and the tens of thousands of jobs lost because of it was because his ex-wife allowed her cousin to take Gigaba's daughter to Cuba to see her, Gigaba gave Tlhabi a very public ultimatum to retract and apologise or face the full wrath of his attorneys.

Tlhabi declined and Gigaba did nothing. But, as the long-suffering public would discover, Gigaba was developing a habit of using state institutions to fight his petty little domestic battles.

Anyway, Gigaba's unmatched ability to act as enabler-in-chief as the Zuptas destroyed our electricity generation system, national airline, railways and ports meant that by 2017 he was destined to attain greater heights. By this time, Zuma was emboldened enough to remove Pravin Gordhan as finance minister, and in his place, the nation was asked to imagine instead that this prick was in our finance ministry... And that, folks, is state capture in action.

There are many contenders for the date that marked the exact nadir of the Zuma administration, but the appointment of Gigaba to head the treasury on 31 March 2017 is a hard one to look past. This was the year that both Standards & Poor's and Fitch downgraded South Africa to sub-investment grade junk status, and Gigaba's permanent visage during his 11 months as finance minister was one of deer-in-the-headlights how-did-I-get-myself-into-this mute horror. He did, however, manage to massage the financial situation as wisely as he could, getting government to okay accumulated travel bills of R870,000+ for his second wife, Norma, as she accompanied him on global roadshows to try to prevent imminent junking of the economy.

Norma was the well- if not long-matched Instagram primping preener who developed a habit of posting pictures of herself spending her taxpayer-funded R16,000 daily allowance in all kinds of bog-ordinary locations that would only ever impress those who've never left Pretoria. It's a fun game, actually, to compare Norma's mortifyingly vain fashion-crime insta-pose nonsense with the ordinary Manhattanites going about their business around her. She looks more of a puffed-up imbecile there than she does here, which is quite a feat.

Malusi and Norma didn't work out, though. Their relationship fell apart not too long after he was forced out of Cabinet (can you believe it). Having been shifted by Cyril Ramaphosa from the finance ministry, in one of the first official moves to try to fix the steaming mess that Zuma had left behind, he was put in charge of Home Affairs once more, but the state capture years of dodgy personal filmography and lying under oath were fast catching up to him. Only weeks after the viral willy wafting emerged, the killer blow was delivered by the Constitutional Court, which denied his bid to overturn an earlier finding that he had told porkies under oath. In that instance, it was in an attempt to allow the Guptas to muscle in on action at OR Tambo after he, as minister of Home Affairs in 2016, had initially approved the Oppenheimer family's private Fireblade terminal. In trying to reverse that decision he found himself up against Nicky Oppenheimer on a hiding to nothing that would eventually see him moved on from Cabinet. That it was one of the richest people in the country who brought about his fall from grace, salary and influence would no doubt have devastated the strutting Gigaba all the more.

"[Gigaba's arguments were] disingenuous, spurious and fundamentally flawed, laboured and meritless, bad in law, astonishing, palpably untrue, untenable and not sustained by objective evidence, uncreditworthy and nonsensical... A court does not readily make findings that a minister's version is untenable and palpably untrue. In this matter it had to be done."

Judge Sulet Potterill of the Pretoria High Court,
ruling against Gigaba in the Fireblade case

The story with Norma still had a little way to run, though. In July 2020 she found herself arrested by the Hawks and thrown in jail overnight for keying a Mercedes-Benz G63. The car in question, with a price tag of around R3.2 million, absolutely didn't belong to Malusi Gigaba, though he was fortunate enough to have friends who lent it to him. And friends who, it seems, could arrange for his wife to be locked up on a Friday afternoon.

One wonders what happens to a man like Gigaba, reduced to bitterly calling in favours from the cops to teach his wife a lesson, as she put it, in yet another public/domestic embarrassment, and arguing in Parliament about penis size with the EFF.

Gigaba is a cautionary tale about integrity and what might have been in more moral times. Swept up with the business-class tickets and the ministerial perks, he forgot that power is fleeting. Now his longer-term fate lies in that of the ANC. If the Zuma/Magashule gangsters prevail, he'll be fine.

If not, we bet he looks great in orange.

See Brian Molefe.

Guan Jiang Guang

Massage parlour owner; mates with a minister; rhino horn trafficker; symbol of the decimation of South Africa's rhino

Dishonourable mention: David Mahlobo

IT MAY BE A POINT WE MAKE TOO OFTEN IN THIS BOOK, but what the hell. The cognitive biases, ideological bubbles and false dichotomies heaped upon the world by the big social media networks in their drive for more monetisable rage are a problem.

Exhibit A would be an internet meme (to use the word correctly, for a change) that did the rounds on the South African internet in the early 20-teens. It was a classic false dichotomy: who cares about a rhinoceros when other really bad shit happens in South Africa?!

How the savants mocked people who put those red rhino horns on the front of their cars. As one smug commentator put it, "When the state gunned down 34 miners in Marikana for asking for a living wage, they were silent." (Also: "the plastic rhino horns look like dildos".)

You could have fun with this wearisome posturing, in a *reductio-ad-absurdum* kind of way. When battery hens were being mistreated, they were silent. When the Chinese continued to occupy Tibet, they were silent. When I was served a dissatisfying Caesar salad at the News Café in Sandton, they were silent. When the French government changed regulations that allowed cheese manufacturers to use the name "Camembert" when the cheese has been made with pasteurised milk, instead of raw milk, they were silent.

"When a terrible thing happened and I needed to clamber over the dead at Marikana to proclaim my virtue, they were silent," seems to be a fairer analysis of this very online, very boring line of argument. Because most adults are actually able to hold two (or more!) unrelated and objectively true facts in their heads at the same time.

You *can* care about both. It's only Twitter's algorithms that don't like it.

And so to the rhinos. They matter a great deal. They are a relic, dinosaurs in a modern world, and they are, for one thing, important to tourism. Far more importantly, though, rhinos are beautiful and, to steal from the philosopher Roger Scruton, "beauty is vanishing from our world because we live as though it did not matter".

It's worth remembering that the first and most devastating rhino poachers were the European settlers. According to veteran wildlife reporter Mic Smith, it is estimated that in East Africa, "170,000 black rhinos were killed for the trade in their horn between 1849 and 1895 to supply 11,000kg/year to Asia". And in South Africa, "the white hunters and their guests shot South Africa almost out of elephant and rhino except for in a few areas, by 1860".

So, before we get too excited about the market for rhino horn as some kind of crude form of Viagra for priapically unimpressive Asian men, let's first get some facts straight. Rhino populations were obliterated by uncontrolled trophy hunting during the colonial era, and the tenuous state of our rhino populations has a lot less to do with Eastern erections, much as some people may like the salaciousness of the idea.

That established, we can surely agree that the shooting and killing of African rhinos for their horns was, and remains, a tragedy for South Africa's natural heritage, whatever the reasons. Those reasons include the buddy-buddy relationship between Jacob Zuma's disastrous Minister of State Security David Mahlobo and a Chinese national by the name of Guan Jiang Guang, who was a known rhino horn smuggler. Known, that is, to everyone except David Mahlobo, which is quite something since Mahlobo was our security minister at the time and Guan was a bona fide self-confessed criminal. But then Mahlobo also claimed he thought he was going to Guan's "spa" which was code for "massage parlour" which was code for brothel. Of course, Guan vanished in a puff of smoke the minute their cosy relationship emerged.

That was all in 2016, with rhino poaching in South Africa at its awful peak, and serpentine syndicates of businessmen, veterinarians and poaching grunts running amok. Between 2013 and 2017 more than a thousand rhinos, out of a population of approximately 20,000, were killed and butchered for their horns each year in the country.

The good news is that, by the end of the decade, it appeared that the tide had turned and we were beginning to win the war against the poachers, with killings declining for a fifth consecutive year. The departure of Mahlobo from Cabinet in 2018 may or may not have been relevant. What absolutely was relevant was the coordinated human effort it took to marshal the forces required to take on the gangsters and smugglers, like Guan, who care nothing for the natural world. It's a response that echoes the efforts of conservation pioneers like Ian Player and Magqubu Ntombela many decades ago, who rescued the white rhino, in particular, from the verge of extinction. Given that South Africa is home to around 80% of the world's rhinos, this is worth celebrating.

Still, far too many rhinos are dying and the war on poaching is far from over. It has distracted SANParks from the difficult business of running our precious national parks, it has brought violent and dangerous people into our natural places, and it has caused harm to our tourism.

> "Beauty is an ultimate value – something that we pursue for its own sake, and for the pursuit of which no further reason need be given. Beauty should therefore be compared to truth and goodness, one member of a trio of ultimate values which justify our rational inclinations."
>
> *Roger Scruton*

But apart from anything else, it's just brutal and inhuman to mow down a rhinoceros with an AK-47 and hack off its horn while it lies there, dying. Surely, even in the post-truth era, we can all agree on that?

The Guptas

*b. in a time when countries were colonised by other
countries, not families (c. the late 1960s)*

*Modern familial colonists; three-headed embodiment
of South African state capture; Zuma's puppeteers*

*Dishonourable mentions: Malusi Gigaba,
Des van Rooyen, Duduzane Zuma, Jacob Zuma,
Mosebenzi Zwane et al*

ALEKSANDR SOLZHENITSYN OBSERVED that you only need a mouthful of
seawater to know the taste of the ocean. With that in mind, consider the
story that shot the Gupta brothers to infamy in South Africa.

In 2013, the niece of Ajay, Atul and Rajesh Gupta was getting married, and the brothers Gupta wanted to put on a show for their friends and family and business associates to remember. They wanted glitz and glamour and excess at the classiest joint they could think of, Sun City, and, perhaps unfortunately for other less-resourceful brothers, they didn't want to pay for it. So they arranged for the South African taxpayer to do so instead; which is to say, they stole money via a government department and assigned portions of that money to cover the wedding costs. They then booked out Sun City for four days, chartered an Airbus to fly in the family from India, and got permission from their friend Jacob Zuma, the President of South Africa, to land it at Waterkloof Air Force Base, a national key point that was conveniently close to their chosen party destination. Illegal blue-light escorts chaperoned them on their last leg of the journey, before they enjoyed "the event of the millennium" with a suitably impressed guest list of ministers, businessmen and peddlers of influence. As a noteworthy aside, the Guptas demanded that the event organisers provide only white waiters, which appears to validate widespread claims that they are anti-black racists.

The amount of money involved in this little heist is hardly eye-watering by state capture standards: a round R30 million. Really not worth getting your panties in a twist about compared to some of the quantities acquired without warrant, blatantly thieved or simply blown out of existence in many other pages of this book. But the Gupta wedding was a revealing event, a garishly wonderful peek into the way the brothers do business. In the words of journalist Richard Poplak, it "was a political event designed to make a political statement: *We own this country*." In hindsight, though, it proved more than even that.

For one, it was the gig that placed the Guptas squarely in the public's eye. Before the wedding, from around 2010, investigative journalists had been probing their questionable relationship with Zuma; they weren't unknown in South Africa, but they weren't really dinner-time conversation either. Afterwards, they certainly were, and eventually they would be "the most hated family in South Africa". The wedding was the link between the two estimations, their debutante ball. Notably, this wasn't for the thievery of the R30 million, details of which would only be revealed much later; it was for the flaunting of their relationship with Zuma, the famous "Number One", who could arrange the use of the country's premier air force base if he sat ever-so-comfortably in your pocket.

Second, the wedding was a who's who of almost all the paid-off, ethically compromised players who had been drawn into the Gupta orbit, and who would in the following years reveal themselves as complicit in the looting of the country. The draft guest list, laughably misspelt as it was, offered some raw insight into the family's ambition. Just about every politician with an inkling of power was spreadsheeted, from the president through the Cabinet to all the premiers, along with dozens of SOE executives, heads of the major banks and the most prominent white monopoly capitalists in the country, Johann Rupert, Jonathan Oppenheimer and Koos Bekker. (Bell Pottinger hadn't been paid to spread the WMC poison just yet, so this wasn't a problem.) They even earmarked spots for well-known journalists "Ferel" Haffajee, "Philisia" Oppelt and Peter Bruce so that, one presumes, the masses might learn of this splendid affair. (In the end, they got a PR company to send out media updates.)

When the time came, discretion got the better of most of those targeted for acquisition, but many prominent figures succumbed to temptation: the dupe they wanted as finance minister *(see Des van Rooyen)*; the dupe they eventually got as finance minister *(see Malusi Gigaba)*; the dupes who would audit for them *(see below)*.

Following the outcry over the Waterkloof landing, Jacob Zuma himself withdrew his RSVP at the last moment, but there were various other Zumas in his stead. The most conspicuous was his slick but pliable son Duduzane, who had been appointed as director of Mabengela Investments, a Gupta company, in 2008. He was only 25 at the time, with no qualifications to speak of bar one: his father had recently become president of the ANC. By 2013 Duduzane was in the process of amassing a fortune in business with the Guptas, and would come to be seen as a greasy nexus between the families; the point of contact between the man with power and the men with money. He appears to have served as inspiration for other children of politicians, not least the Magashule boys, to head down the slippery slope to where business meets political influence.

Which leads us to the Gupta wedding's third insight: the mechanics of the job. In this instance, the basics required were a morally flexible contact in the department of agriculture of a friendly province, a bogus dairy project, a few front companies to launder the money, and an amenable transnational auditor – really, not much more than that.

The Guptas' key man here was one Mosebenzi Zwane, another wedding attendee, who was MEC for Agriculture and Rural Development for one of Zuma's key men, Premier of the Free State Ace Magashule. Zwane helped set up a dairy project near his home town of Vrede and award the contract, worth R114 million, to Estina (Pty) Ltd, a company wholly unqualified for the job. The project would, however, never get going: a plot of land was leased, the poor locals were sold some promises of a better life, and that was about it. Instead, the bulk of the money was transferred to a Gupta-run shell company in Dubai and then laundered back into South Africa via several more Gupta shells.

One company in particular, Linkway Trading, ended up receiving exactly R30 million from another company, Accurate Investments Limited. The invoice in question described the payment for "V&A Function", which happened to be the initials of Vega and Aakash, the bride and groom at the wedding in question. All that was left to do was for the Guptas' auditors, KPMG, to look the other way as they signed

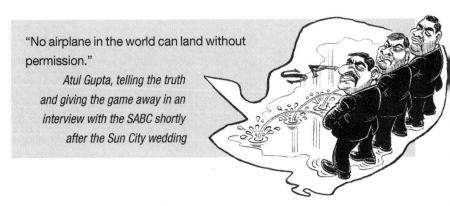

"No airplane in the world can land without permission."
Atul Gupta, telling the truth and giving the game away in an interview with the SABC shortly after the Sun City wedding

off, which they did by pretending that Accurate and Linkway were unrelated parties. They no doubt considered this a fair trade for their wedding invites.

And, lo, the deed was done.

The brazenness of it all defines the process. Just as they set up a newspaper and news channel – *The New Age* and ANN7 – that were quite clearly their propaganda outlets from day one, so the Vrede-dairy-farm-as-wedding-fund was exactly what it looked like. They felt no need to set up a rudimentary dairy project as cover. They couldn't be bothered to come up with a less crackable reference than "V&A Function". The auditors even wrote off the whole thing as a business expense: no taxes paid on the stolen tax money – now that's tax optimisation, boys! For the Guptas, by now ensconced as the family behind the people who ran South Africa, repercussions were the merest hypothetical.

And hey, wasn't it a cracking party? Invoices that formed part of the Gupta Leaks revealed that very nearly half a million bucks went on booze alone. It does raise the question: if you steal money, does it by some poorly understood course of nature mean that you must be *completely* tasteless? Had the Guptas actually earned the R30 million they blew on this wedding, one wonders whether it might have been an iota less nauseating. Might they have looked at the cost of the harpists, for example, or the scale of the fireworks display (invoiced cost: R300,000) and thought, you know, let's turn this down a bit? Maybe this is just ever so slightly disgusting?

Now, drink up that seawater and imagine this vignette played out again and again and again. Imagine that the Guptas hadn't merely "captured" a provincial farming project, but an entire country, its senior politicians and its treasury; that the R30 million wedding really is a mouthful of pilfering compared to the ocean of thievery in which the Gupta brothers swim. Well, no need to imagine; just page through any number of entries in this book.

By some estimates, these émigrés – apparently despatched by their father from India in the early 1990s to "take advantage" of the opportunities that might arise in the country's new political era – have acquired somewhere in the region of a hundred billion rand in their rigging of tenders, plundering of state apparatus and effective insider-trading as a result of their relationship with the president of the country. But "a hundred billion rand" is one of those thumbsuck guesstimates that does no justice to the enormity of the damage they've wrought. For they haven't stolen mere money from the South African people; they've stolen years from its economic trajectory and even the lives of its citizens. They've destabilised the entire country, torn its ruling party to pieces, sewn noxious racial discord among its people (as we saw a couple of entries ago), rendered ineffective whole ministries and SOEs. They've thrown a generation of mainly black South Africans under the bus and, when it all came to a head and they began to reap the whirlwind of public then journalistic then finally political retribution, they skipped abroad with their loot piled high in the private jet. That was April 2016.

The Guptas left wholesale destruction in their wake – those who had presumed a Zuma presidency would be corrupt and disastrous way back in 2009 could not have imagined this. But the moment they left was also the moment a pinprick of hope revealed itself to the country. And it was the moment Zuma was suddenly no longer untouchable.

Today, with a new NPA in place, we would very much like to encourage the Guptas to return.

John Hlophe

b. 19 May 1959

*Judge President of the Western Cape; South Africa's most
controversial judge; embodiment of the Stalingrad legal
defence; judicial credibility killer; victim player;
the lower standard*

Dishonourable mentions: Michael Hulley, Jacob Zuma

INNOCENT UNTIL PROVEN GUILTY.

Right?

We live in an age when this fundamental tenet of the liberal justice
system is seen to be at risk in so many spheres of life, in particular those
described and amplified on social media. Modern-day witch-hunts

by Twitter require the merest suggestion of improper behaviour or impure thought for the accused to be harangued, bullied or targeted for cancellation by self-imposed enforcers of moral virtue.

There was early Twitter-mob victim Justine Sacco, a South African working in New York who, while on a flight from London to Cape Town in 2013, was denounced by the social media hive mind, which then created a hashtag dedicated to having her fired before her plane landed. She had told a bad joke.*

There was the philosopher Roger Scruton (referenced a few pages back), who was sacked from a UK government advisory position in 2019 in response to a social media uproar because of remarks he had made that were deemed intolerant. His quotes had been deliberately taken out of context by a journalist, and he later received an apology from government and was reinstated.

More recently and famously, there is JK Rowling, who has been designated a TERF (trans-exclusionary radical feminist), denounced by many of the actors whose careers she helped launch, and sent dozens of death threats. This, most notably, after she had objected to the term "people who menstruate" in a tweet.

In South Africa, the accusations of Salem are most pronounced when the charge has anything to with race. If you're H&M or Clicks, for instance, and you don't quality-control your advertisements, you may find your stores trashed by EFF trolls the next day – which happened in January 2018 to the former and September 2020 to the latter. Accused, tried and sentenced with just one tweet from above. No mitigating circumstances here.

Though the real-world effects are dramatic and life-affecting in these cases and others like them, notice, please, that none of this is actual judicial justice. Thankfully, the notion of innocent until proven guilty is something we still adhere to in our liberal democracy, a tenet that

---

* Sacco was fired shortly after landing, and spent a year trying to get her career back on track. Her offending tweet, sent from Heathrow Airport, read, "Going to Africa. Hope I don't get Aids. Just kidding. I'm white!"

underscores the very fabric of modern civilisation. Without it you may as well live in a Kafka novel.

So we'll draw our line in the sand here. John Hlophe is innocent of any crime until proven guilty. But we have to say, it's not looking good for him.

* * * *

In a microcosm of modern existence, the court of popular justice and the court of actual justice swing from one extreme to the other. On social and even mainstream media: instant, often wildly misguided mob verdicts. In South African courts of law: painfully drawn-out and politicised legal wrangles seemingly without any verdicts.

In recent years we've acquired a dedicated term for the latter phenomenon – the Stalingrad defence, in which a defendant's vast legal team obfuscates, prevaricates, procrastinates and discombobulates, using all the legal tricks of the trade to kick a case's can down the road. *Ab initio, inter alia*, they object to matters of procedure and personnel, apply for stays of prosecution, change legal representatives, encourage "extraneous litigation", call in sick, appeal all verdicts, delay and postpone, postpone and delay, *bovis stercus ad infinitum*. Basically, it's professional ducking and diving to ensure your client never has his day in court. Ideally for the proponent, it goes on until someone somewhere gets the case thrown out. And it's given that much more room to play out in South Africa because of the sorry state of the NPA which, even when it isn't being actively influenced from above, is under so much operational pressure that regular delays from its side are inevitable.

The most prominent proponent of the Stalingrad defence is, of course, Jacob Zuma, who used it, under the guidance of his legal field marshal Michael Hulley, with such effect that it bridged his entire presidency. He could be president of a country of 50 million people with grave charges of fraud and money laundering hanging over his head because innocent until proven guilty, your honour. Charges of corruption relating to the Arms Deal were first brought against Zuma in 2005, the same year that Schabir Shaik was convicted in a separate trial and sent to prison for being in a corrupt relationship with him. The logic of it all seemed fairly watertight: Schabir Shaik was guilty of being in a corrupt relationship with Jacob Zuma, therefore Jacob Zuma was... Fast-forward 15 years and we still don't have an official answer.

For some insight into the practicalities of these things, consider more recent events in the case. In May 2019, a stay of prosecution application by Zuma and his co-accused, the French arms manufacturer Thales, was heard in the KwaZulu-Natal High Court. It took until October of that year for the full bench of three judges to reach and declare its verdict, which was that the application should be dismissed and the corruption trial should continue. With the actual trial of Zuma due to commence within days of the announcement, political commentators optimistically wondered whether the Stalingrad strategy had finally been defeated. But, as if by magic, a year slid on by, and by the following September there had been no meaningful progress, to the point that the Jacob Zuma Foundation could issue a statement claiming that inadequacies at the NPA were unfairly delaying the hearing of the case. (One of the clearest indicators that the Stalingrad strategy is being deployed is when the suspect boldly makes it known that he wants his day in court, a proposition that is entirely at odds with all other evidence.)

So we see that Zuma, still innocent after all these years, has proved to be something of a contemporary legal pioneer. Today we see his strategy reflected across many political cases, notably in the way ANC Secretary-General Ace Magashule merrily defends party officials who face accusations of corruption but have yet to face the sticky end of a trial. Recent examples include ANC Limpopo treasurer Danny Msiza and deputy chairperson Florence Radzilani, both implicated in the VBS Mutual Bank scandal – and in defending them, he is effectively defending himself. Remember, innocent until proven blah blah... Now let us all get back to work on the taxpayer's dime.

Ace and the cadres have been shown the magic trick and they'll keep using it, because a precedent has been set and there is evidently no viable counter-strategy.

* * * *

The Stalingrad defence isn't just at play on the political battlefield. We see it in business, in our local homeowners' association disputes and, perhaps most worryingly, in our precious judiciary. One of our finest proponents of the strategy is also one of the most senior legal figures in the land: Judge President of the Western Cape Division of the High Court of South Africa, John Hlophe. In a sense, much of Hlophe's career has been a Stalingrad defence, with accusations of all sorts going back nearly two decades.

Appointed Judge President in 2000, Hlophe was considered an especially bright young star of the South African judiciary. His background was truly something. Born at the height of apartheid in Madundube, a rural backwater in northern KwaZulu-Natal, the story goes that he was identified by the local farmer's wife as the brightest kid in the area and sent off to Prospect Farm Primary School. It was a vanishingly rare opportunity for the child of a traditional healer and a sugar-cane cutter to make something of himself, and it was the first step that ultimately saw him becoming a Cambridge scholarship winner and a potential future Chief Justice of South Africa. A helluva tale.

But about four years into his role as Judge President, the epic trajectory he was following seems to have veered off course, and he has been served the full breakfast buffet of allegations since: misconduct, corruption, defamation, nepotism, racism, playing the race card, disparaging colleagues, creating a "climate of fear and intimidation", assault, abuse, aggression, sexual impropriety and essentially being an incorrigible asshole. In late 2020 he even faced the surely ludicrous accusation of being involved in a plot to assassinate his deputy, Patricia Goliath. Then again, the list of other high-profile judges he has publicly and often splenetically butted heads with include Dikgang Moseneke, Johann Kriegler, Jeanette Traverso, Edwin King, Pius Langa and Mogoeng Mogoeng – the latter two while they were Chief Justices.

Hlophe is the most senior judge in the Western Cape, and should be a rock of calm, authority and morality, above reproach. And yet his life and career reads, as *Business Day* reporter Karyn Maughan puts it, "like a long-running soap opera: sensational, interminable and even repetitive".

Of Hlophe's many notable controversies, the most public and potentially ruinous, both to him and the reputation of our courts, is the 2008 allegation that he attempted to influence two judges, Bess Nkabinde and Chris Jaftha, to ensure a Constitutional Court ruling went in favour of Jacob Zuma. As a result, he has faced impeachment on the matter for all of 12 years and counting, interminably delayed by ongoing legal challenges, and mixed in with other scandal, including an obscure dispute between Environment Minister Barbara Creecy and Hlophe's attorney Barnabas Xulu.

Unsurprisingly, Hlophe categorically denies it all, and again he has followed Zuma's lead, playing the persecution card on a regular basis. He's not the bad guy, folks, he's the victim. Innocent until blah.

Here's the thing. Whether he is innocent or guilty, victim or villain, is now well besides the point. For people in position of great authority, there is critical need for a culture of "higher standard" to apply. If your reputation is brought into disrepute, you should stand down while you defend your name, and in so doing protect the integrity of the institution you represent.

Sadly, our lost decade offers perilously few examples of high-profile public figures who have done the right thing and stood down for causing controversy and impugning the reputation of a state institution. We count one: Nhlanhla Nene, who resigned from the position of minister of finance in October 2018, when he admitted to having meetings with the Guptas that he had previously denied. These weren't criminal offences in themselves, but he did the decent thing – unlike Hlophe, Zuma, Magashule and the cadres who take their cues from above.

"'Innocent until proven guilty' indeed appears to mean 'innocent until the last avenue of appeal has been exhausted'. While that could be a good working requirement for mafia bosses, surely that should not be a standard that the aspirant leaders of our society should adhere to?"

Stephen Grootes, September 2020

"The impropriety of the judge president's insistence on occupying the office while accused of such a serious charge is all the greater. The suspicion alone disqualifies him. The judge president has no more right to continue in judicial office than a suspected paedophile has to continue running a nursery school."

Justice Johann Kriegler, writing in February 2009

"Prompt and transparent action is needed to dissipate the toxic atmosphere on the Western Cape Bench. Manifestly the starting point – and hopefully the solution – is the urgent removal of the judge president... The problem created by Judge Hlophe has to be confronted once and for all. Every day of inaction that passes further erodes public faith and optimism."

Justice Johann Kriegler, writing in February 2020 about exactly the same case

This book is about the opportunities forgone in our "lost" last decade. If ever it needed a metaphor, it is the ongoing principal legal cases against Zuma and Hlophe – both started before the decade began and both will end, if they ever end, well after it has finished. Judge Hlophe, in particular, ultimately comes to epitomise the legal maxim that "justice delayed is justice denied". In his case, the justice is to the South African public, who have watched the integrity of the country's courts shudder and strain in crisis as the system struggles to hold itself accountable. "Teflon John", as he has come to be known, remains technically clean after all these years, but has proved to be a deep smear on our judiciary to the detriment of us all.

There is, however, a glimmer of hope. As effective as it is, South Africans recently discovered that the Stalingrad defence is not entirely impervious to the steady assault of process over time. After 21 years of stalling and evasion, one of the ropiest fellows of our post-democratic history, former spy chief Richard Mdluli, was finally convicted for kidnapping and assault in September 2020. It wasn't the murder conviction it might have been, given that the man he assaulted in 1999 later ended up shot dead, and he was yet to be cheered into prison by an ANC send-off party by the time this book went to print, but a fortress of injustice had finally been penetrated.

Zuma, Hlophe and their fellow strategists would, we hope, have read the news in their foxholes with some concern.

Trevor Hoole
& friends

*Disgraced ex-employees of KPMG; usually nameless
suits who enabled massive corporate and political fraud;
representatives of the failure of Big Four auditing*

Dishonourable mentions: Sipho Malaba, Jacques Wessels

IN ITS EXCELLENT REPORT "THE AUDITORS", Open Secrets unleashed
this little gem onto the world:

"In 2016, in South Africa, 25% of the JSE's top 40 companies
appointed individuals who were previously employed by their
external auditors as chairperson of their audit committees."

Indeed, this convenient cosiness between corporations and their supposedly independent auditors is a structural problem faced by the global economy, a problem that might relatively easily be fixed if anyone had the appetite for it.

As much as one may bring an auditor's "professional scepticism" to the lefty capitalism-is-evil tone of "The Auditors", the fact is that Deloitte had audited Murray & Roberts, the building giant, for 117 years prior to the regulator enforcing mandatory rotation. Deloitte had also looked after Tongaat Hulett for 82 years.

It requires not an iota of anti-capitalist sentiment to see the problem here. If you've been with somebody for 117 years, or even a mere 82, it's gone beyond a transactional relationship. You're a couple, co-dependent, joined at the hip. There are no secrets between you and you see past each other's flaws. In elderly humans this is all rather sweet, but on the JSE – where the pensions of real elderly people reside – it's problematic, to say the least.

Well, they don't seem bothered at the gleaming head office of Giganticorp, Sandton. The incredibly slick annual-results presentations with messages sharply honed by the best communications experts in the country, the interim reports, the quarterly sales figures, the balance sheets and the cash positions – all are signed off by their "independent" auditor, with whom they've been sharing pillow talk since early last century. And all are used in good faith by asset managers and pension fund administrators to help them decide where to store the meagre wealth earned in a lifetime of hard work by nurses, cops and street sweepers.

When Murray & Roberts was fined more than R370 million by the Competition Commission for sector collusion relating to construction projects for the 2010 Soccer World Cup, one would hope that the auditors were genuinely not to blame – but might they have kept a sharper lookout without a century's relationship to obscure the view? And how do we explain Tongaat Hulett overstating its assets by more than R10 billion without mentioning the bean counters?

The authors of the "The Auditors" adopt a legitimately furious tone, and are quick to ensure the reader understands that the cosy arrangements between the Big Four accounting firms – Deloitte, KPMG, EY and PwC – and their clients are enormously dangerous, and have already caused significant economic harm. After all, if strict processes are muddied with personal relationships and institutional intimacy, it takes just one bad apple and the whole barrel can be poisoned.

Before we get into that, "one bad apple" is best written as "one bad auditing apple", because, as has been observed elsewhere, it takes two to tango. JSE regulations and auditing requirements exist because there is a regulatory presumption that businesspeople will – if you'll excuse some straight talking – take the piss, cut corners and generally make themselves look better than they are. We know that people like Markus Jooste exist and invariably find their way to the top of the corporate tree, and that's why we don't let them count their own beans.

Anybody who's ever experienced a proper corporate audit will adopt the Border War 1,000-yard stare and tell you how tough it is. Real auditors are simply relentless. They miss nothing. Loose auditing, though, is like corruption. Once you've let one thing slide, they've got you. Until the day you die, *you will have let that one thing slide*, and it will forever be something those who benefited from this act of laissez-faire auditing can use against you as leverage for future auditing largesse.

It's thin-edge-of-the-wedge stuff. Because soon enough, loose auditing *is* corruption. One "Let's carry that small cost into the next fiscal because then I'll make target and get an additional 50% bonus" can, with the same auditor, quickly unravel into something like, "How about we pay you R23 million for a report that says what we tell you to say?" We can't say for sure that that's how Tom Moyane's relationship with KPMG started out, but that's certainly where it ended up when the auditor delivered its fabricated report on the SARS "rogue unit".

With the Big Four making up more than 99% of accounting services for the top 500 companies on the Nasdaq, and 100% in the FTSE top 100, this risk is, as the analysts say, almost baked in. There has been scandal after scandal, but South Africa, where graft is the only operating system the government understands, where inequality is stark, where the grey area between those who survive and those who starve is a populous locale, and where the lifeline that measly pensions offer is so critical, there was perhaps a perfect vacuum of vulnerability.

The crime of the auditors is that they are the Great Enablers. The supposedly upstanding pillars of Castle Capital's very existence are supposed to ensure the protection of the smallest shareholders from the depredations of the Sandton charlatans in their Hugo Boss suits, BMW M-what-whats and other accoutrements of New Money. Instead, the auditors burned their clipboards and asked for the tailor's contact details.

The sense that grand-scale corruption is the purlieu of the government and the state's businesses is troublesome. This untrue idea serves as grist to the anti-black racists' mill. It serves those who hate the ANC for other reasons. Equally, it creates space for white white-collar criminals to operate with even more impunity than their black state-employed brethren. And, finally, it allows the state capturers to ask (with reason) why the hell Markus Jooste is not in jail. Regrettably, it allows them to conclude (without reason) that it is because he is white. Twitter sock puppets and bots paid for by the gangsters are only too happy to amplify this nonsense.

> "It is hard to accept that an alert external auditor, using proper standards of professional scepticism and common sense, and with insight into all of Steinhoff's accounts, should not have raised red flags earlier."
> *Open Secrets, on Deloitte's failure to detect Steinhoff's R106 billion fraud*

There is no space here to go into the many scandals and failures of the Big Four around the world, from Enron to Lehman Brothers. They have jointly signed off on the most appalling theft and destruction of value, and there is some succour to be had in knowing we have not been specifically neglected in South Africa. But neglected we have been, most notably in recent years. Deloitte didn't spot R106 billion worth of fraud committed over many years at Steinhoff. PwC missed numerous problems at SAA. KPMG signed off on the SARS "rogue unit" report, the Gupta wedding at Sun City as financed by the Vrede/Estina dairy project, and the looting of funds at VBS Mutual Bank.

That first one was a biggie, which is why we have an entry dedicated to Markus Jooste. In short, if you have a pension scheme, chances are you were a Steinhoff shareholder. Nearly a thousand schemes held stock. The value of that particular investment has plummeted 98% and has cost state workers alone – that's the nurses and cops and street sweepers – a cool R21 billion.

But it isn't always easy for the average observer to make sense of the accounting shenanigans that see unfathomable sums of money vanishing into the ether. They are derelictions of duty, and occasionally crimes, that seem to exist in another dimension; the interactions of nameless, faceless suits behind gleaming glass edifices in Sandton or Midrand. Somewhere along the line a fine of many millions may be paid but then it seems to be business/accounting as usual.

So let's put a few names to them. Let's call out some of the individuals involved, the bad apples. Let's talk about Trevor, Jacques and Sipho, and their colleagues Steven, Ahmed, Mike, Muhammad, Herman, Johan and Mickey, all former employees at KPMG.

There is something vomit-inducing about the way state capture and old-fashioned robbery was enabled, to put it mildly, by Trevor Hoole, Jacques Wessels and Sipho Malaba. In the first case, Hoole was the CEO of KPMG South Africa who evaded the tough questions as it became increasingly evident that the SARS "rogue unit" report that his company had put together was more than a little mistaken. It was, in fact, a sham that was composed, almost word for word in places, of what Jacob Zuma's lieutenant Tom Moyane wanted it to be composed of. To protect Zuma and his cronies, it would lead to the unjustified firing of 50 SARS officials, and cause incalculable damage to the state's ability to collect taxes. When KPMG finally acknowledged its complicity and retracted its findings in September 2017, Hoole was forced to resign, along with seven others, who we'll name here just in case you ever happen to find yourself attending a dinner party in their presence. They were COO Steven Louw, chairman of the board Ahmed Jaffer, and senior

> "KPMG South Africa CEO Trevor Hoole is at best a man who has looked the other way as his associates undertake work that enriches and empowers the Zupta clique, transforming South Africa into a kleptocracy. The KPMG name has popped up with increasing frequency wherever there is the smell of state capture and corruption."
>
> *Thulisizwe Sithole, 2017*

executives Mike Oddy, Muhammad Saloojee, Herman de Beer, Johan Geel and Mickey Bove.

Jacques Wessels, meanwhile, was the grease that lubricated the wheels of the Gupta family's looting of the Vrede/Estina dairy project so that one of their daughters might have a glamorous wedding. It's a sorry affair we covered two entries back. For his efforts, Wessels cracked the nod to the wedding in 2013 and was barred from practising as an auditor in 2019.

Finally, to Sipho Malaba, the auditor arrested in connection with the looting of more than R2 billion from VBS Mutual Bank, a bank created specifically to cater to the poorest of poor South Africans. It has been widely reported that Malaba received more than R30 million of the savings cash and illegally deposited municipal funds that the VBS thieves enlisted him to sanitise with a KPMG sign-off. You'd think a salary of more than R2.5 million would be enough to compensate you for the work of protecting the poor, but evidently Malaba had a pressing need to have a Range Rover, Land Rover *and* Mercedes-Benzes in his Fourways driveway.

In Malaba's case, it appears that a trainee auditor at KPMG first sounded the alarm that the numbers weren't adding up, which would suggest that some of the nameless, faceless suits at the auditors are still good apples. Best we do what we can to look after them and weed out the rotten ones.

See The Guptas, Markus Jooste, Tom Moyane, Dudu Myeni, Floyd Shivambu.

Thamsanqa Jantjie

b. 1979

*Dabbler in necklacing and mob justice; frequenter of
mental health facilities; sign-language interpreter unable
to do sign-language interpreting; victim of South African
state incompetence*

IN 2003, AN INFURIATED COMMUNITY caught two men with stolen
televisions and, in that South African way, they took it upon themselves
to necklace them.

"It was a community thing, what you call mob justice, and I was also
there," Thamsanqa Jantjie told the *Sunday Times*. Jantjie would never face
trial for the murders, as others did, as he was apparently not considered
mentally fit to stand trial. He was instead institutionalised for a year.

Jump ahead to 10 December 2013, and South Africa was at the epicentre of a rare and poignant global moment. Nelson Mandela, the icon, had died, and the world's attention was focused on Soccer City in Johannesburg for the most important state memorial service in our country's history.

South Africa had been readying for some time for the passing of its first democratic president and the colossus of modern world history. The newspapers had been prepared, the columns written, the pictures chosen, the analysis done and dusted. The details of his funeral, his lying in state, and the accompanying events, had been hashed out years in advance, with the input of Mandela himself. Preparations had been made for the arrival of more than a hundred heads of state and 50 former heads of state; of kings, queens, princes and princesses.

This was our moment. We had this.

So quite how a mentally unwell mob-murder participant was called only the day before to handle the sign-language interpretation, we can only imagine. This was, it turns out, a man who had recently suffered a relapse, but who delayed a scheduled admission to the Sterkfontein Psychiatric Hospital when the opportunity arose to attend the service. For a man in a fragile state of mind, it's hard to imagine a more intimidating request. And yet there was Thamsanqa Jantjie, standing but a metre from US President Barack Obama, UN Secretary-General Ban Ki-moon and an array of world leaders as they delivered their eulogies, flailing his arms about in an utterly incomprehensible last-guy-on-the-dance-floor-at-3am manner while, as he would explain it, hallucinating about angels flying about the stadium.

"I don't remember any of this at all," he said to the Associated Press when shown footage of himself on stage.

The deaf community was understandably appalled, as the eulogies were rendered meaningless by Jantjie's nonsensical signing. The Americans were flabbergasted – formally they were "upset" – that a man with Jantjie's history and who admits to suffering from bouts of violence had managed to get anywhere near Obama. Somehow, South Africa had fluffed its lines on the grandest stage imaginable.

Nobody can be held accountable for their own illness, but Jantjie was the worst possible guy in the wrong place at a critical moment. In time, an apology from government was forthcoming, though it was couched, not unexpectedly, in begrudging indifference and evasion. "When somebody provides a service of a sign-language interpreter," said Deputy Disability Minister Hendrietta Bogopane-Zulu, "I don't think… somebody would say: 'Is your head okay? Do you have any mental disability?' I think the focus was on: 'Are you able to sign? Can you provide the services?'"

Except that he wasn't able to sign, was he?

Bogopane-Zulu apologised to the deaf community but said there was no reason for the country to be embarrassed.

Of course not. Nothing to see here. Just par for the course.

Markus Jooste

b. 22 January 1961

CEO of Steinhoff International (2000-2017);
Stellenbosch mafioso; irregular accountant; insider trader;
swarthy face of corporate malfeasance; most loathed
businessman in South Africa?

IF ENTITLEMENT IS OUR GREAT DISEASE, then that can only leave Marcus Jooste as some kind of national super-spreader. Jooste was, until 2017, the CEO of Steinhoff International, and we believe he is a very bad man indeed. For what it's worth, he is also sensationally unlikeable.

Spokesman for the National Prosecuting Authority (NPA) Sipho Ngwema promises that Jooste will get his day in court one day, but in the meantime we are left to ponder the startling injustice of that day not coming sooner than it will. Indeed, why it hasn't come already. This is yet another consequence of the damage inflicted upon South Africa through the NPA's capture by the Zupta ghouls, as outlined in the first entry in the book. *(See Shaun Abrahams.)*

Steal a loaf of bread from Pick n Pay and the police will come and you will go to court and you'll be sentenced in a month. Steal hundreds of millions of rands or destroy the wealth of many people at an astonishing scale, and there just isn't the capacity at the NPA to handle the complexities of the case. Three years after the collapse of Steinhoff due to "accounting irregularities", Jooste still roams the streets of Stellenbosch and Hermanus without having faced a prosecutor.

It's important to understand that the NPA's dearth of prosecutors with the skills to take on the Steinhoff case, and Jooste's enduring freedom, are not some kind of indicator of the lack of severity of the crime. Let us not make this mistake. If state capture and government corruption is deplorable because public funds are supposed to work to our collective benefit, then those directors of listed companies hold in their hands private money that is even harder-earned than it might have been. Any kind of corporate fraud or negligence on top of the already existing government fraud or negligence thus becomes a double whammy. It is the decimation of the scant funds that people are able to save *after* paying tax, and *after* paying for the consequences of their tax being stolen.

So, once you've paid your income tax, your VAT, your rates and your development levies, and your sin taxes (as you drink to forget the trauma of trying to make ends meet in this country); once you've settled your eye-watering transfer duty and made provisions for the death tax you will pay when you die, only then can you start to pay for things that you have just (supposedly) paid for. And so you will pay to educate your children in a manner that means they will be able to read and count; you will pay for your own private police force because ADT actually works; you will pay for your healthcare because you don't want to die of thirst in a state hospital in a puddle of urine (*see Qedani Mahlangu*).

And only *then*, when you've paid for all that stuff twice, can you invest some money into the stock market. For most people, this is done on your behalf by a Jaguar-driving incompetent (*see The fund manager*) in Cape Town via your pension fund, which also comes with its own special tax. (They prefer the word "fees" but, as with taxes, it's not like you have a choice in the matter.) Here we come to the critical point.

What happens on the JSE is not only a rich person's worry. It's not even restricted to "middle-class problems" and above. This is the post-tax and post-second-tax, post-fund-manager-fees savings of pretty much anyone with a formal job, especially in the state sector where pension savings are, sadly, so often the only savings.

So we should always remember who got hurt most in 2017 after Deloitte refused to sign off Steinhoff's books, starting a cascade of revelations that boggled markets and minds alike and saw upwards of R100 billion evaporate.

Jooste's rise was impressive. He came from relatively little, had to go into significant debt to fund his chartered accounting degree, and quickly roared onto the business track, ambition flowing. In 1988 he helped put together the sale of a South African retail chain to Steinhoff's German owner, and by 2000 he was CEO of the company.

"Markus Jooste has transformed the South African manufacturer into 'Africa's Ikea' and the second-largest household goods retailer in Europe," gushed *Forbes* years later, before explaining that Steinhoff had purchased Pepkor Holdings for $5.7 billion in 2014.

But if Steinhoff's growth was stratospheric then its subsequent downfall was like a meteor crashing to earth. In December 2017 it shed 90% of its value in just a few days. The heavily invested former dollar billionaire Christo Wiese alone lost somewhere in the region of R50 billion. Steinhoff was found to have "released misleading information into the marketplace": it had overstated assets and profits to the tune of $12 billion. It was a staggeringly huge fraud, and the company was fined accordingly by the Financial Sector Conduct Authority (FSCA).

It would take nearly three years before Jooste faced any form of punishment in his personal capacity. In October 2020 the FSCA fined him at least R122 million for advising four Steinhoff shareholders to sell their stock before the shit officially hit the fan. But, as hefty a fine as that may be – the largest the FSCA has ever issued for insider trading – it is really a sideshow. The dodgy accounting itself has not been dealt with.

It will all come to court, one day, and much of the argument will be technical and indecipherable, as those in the world of finance like to keep it. We will follow it in the news, but our eyes will glaze over as the sterile details emerge, as will the eyes of the state workers, the teachers, the policemen, the nurses. (Christo Wiese may stay a little more attentive, but even he will acknowledge that these are the people most deeply affected.) The Government Employees Pension Fund (GEPF), South Africa's biggest pension fund, with R1.8 trillion belonging to 1.7 million current and retired state workers under management, is facing a R12 billion impairment, at least, from the disaster. This after lending an empowerment vehicle with links to Cosatu almost R10 billion to buy shares in Steinhoff. In those days, the share was trading at around R80 a share. Today it's a penny stock, with a "value", at the time of writing, of about 80 cents or so.

Deloitte, it is worth noting, had signed off at least two annual reports, in 2015 and 2016, that were, it appears, not representative of the truth, illustrating once more that it is not only the players who can be at fault, but the referees too.

Jooste quit the firm soon after the bombshell, and has lawyered up and hunkered down in his Stellenbosch laager, waiting for the weakened NPA to make its move. His Bentley Bentayga is sometimes seen cruising Hermanus, where his compound was the target of graffitied insults for a long while, so he's hardly under house arrest, but one would hope that his social circle has shrunk somewhat. He also faced "revelations" of marital infidelity in the aftermath: salacious tales of a much-younger kept woman who drove a matching Bentayga – some kind of polo-playing South Africanised wannabe Barbara Cartland-style cliché. For God's sake. Behind it all there's just a naked emperor riding a donkey.

"Steinhoff is going to struggle to process all the bad news in America for a long time, so there are better places to invest your money, immediately take the current price and delete this SMS and don't call anyone."
Text message from Markus Jooste to four Steinhoff shareholders the week before the irregular accounting scandal broke, as reported in the Financial Mail

Jooste exists in these pages for the scale of the Steinhoff hit on the savings and pensions of ordinary people, money intended to sustain the elderly in the evening of life, give their kids a fighting chance and allow them to spoil their grandchildren. Money for school fees and trips to the beach. To pay for uniforms and food and electricity bills.

He exists here, too, as the representative of corporate fraud: the stereotypical, philandering big-shot businessman who feels entitled to whatever he sets his eye on because who gives a toss for the little people (and Christo Wiese)? The exact person, along with the crooked politician, the world could do without.

And on that note, Jooste exists here also to make the point that listed businesses have public obligations, and that smart-looking businessmen in expensive suits are no more to be trusted than dressed-down politicians in ANC T-shirts.

The sorry story of Steinhoff's implosion on Jooste's watch reminds us of the importance of maintaining institutions and systems that police everyone who handles other people's wealth, be they the Gauteng Department of Health or a Steinhoff International. Now, as with the crooked politicians, we await Markus Jooste's day in court.